C000005711

edges

Assessment for Learning in English

Lindsay McNab

Imelda Pilgrim

Marian Slee

Series consultant: Susan Sutton

2

www.heinemann.co.uk
✓ Free online support
✓ Useful weblinks
✓ 24 hour online ordering

01865 888058

Heinemann

Inspiring generations

Contents

The following icons are used in this book:

 This indicates that **next steps** activities and teaching notes are available in the Assessment and Resource File 2 and Teacher's Handbook 2.

 This indicates that a supplementary activity, or worksheet to support a Student Book activity, is available in the Assessment and Resource File 2.

Introduction

The whole picture

In this book you will explore how writers write, readers read, speakers speak and listeners listen. You will develop skills in assessing your own learning and working out what you need to do to make good progress. By the end of the book we hope you will feel in control and ready to move on.

WHAT? **You will:**
- become a sharper and more perceptive reader and researcher
- develop your talents as a writer
- gain confidence and skill as a speaker and a listener
- take control of your own learning

HOW? **by:**
- reading and researching a range of lively, interesting, focused texts
- experimenting with different note-making methods, writing styles and techniques
- working with other students in formal and informal situations
- assessing your work and using the feedback and progress checks to track your learning and set your own targets

WHY? **because:**
- better reading and research skills help you understand and interpret your world
- writing is an important form of communication
- increasing your confidence in speaking and listening helps you deal effectively with different situations
- when you know what you are learning, and why you are learning it, you make better progress

1 Playing with words

The bigger picture

In this unit you will learn about the differences between language from the past and the present day. By studying a range of texts you will learn about how language changes. You will explore poetry, media texts and the language of advertising to find out how words can be used for different purposes. At the end of the unit you will write a leaflet called 'Words are fun', based on what you have learnt.

WHAT? You will:
- learn to recognise the differences between texts from the past and the present day
- study texts written in standard English and dialect
- investigate some of the techniques used by writers to make an impact on their readers

HOW? by:
- comparing a range of texts from the eighth century to the present
- exploring the links between language and identity
- examining the techniques writers use to get readers' attention
- experimenting with different ways of getting readers' attention

WHY? because:
- looking at texts from the past helps you to understand how English has developed into the English you use today
- thinking about the links between language and identity will help you to express your personality in the way you write
- understanding how writers choose their words helps you to improve your own writing.

Changing English

The English we speak has undergone many changes throughout the centuries and is still changing. You are going to examine several texts which will show you some of the ways in which English has changed and developed over the years.

Activity 1

1 With a partner, read Texts 1–5. Try to work out what each one is about.

2 Put them in the date order you think they were written in. Begin by identifying the text which you think is most recent and work backwards. It will help if you look closely at:

- the spelling

- words you recognise but which have a different meaning in the text

- words you do not recognise at all.

1

'Now sires,'quod he, 'if that yow be so leef
To fynde Deeth, turne up this croked wey,
For in that grove I lafte hym, by my fey,
Under a tree, and there he wole abyde.'

2

By gods me: I marvel what pleasure or felicitie they have in taking this rogish Tabacco: it's good for nothing but to choke a man.

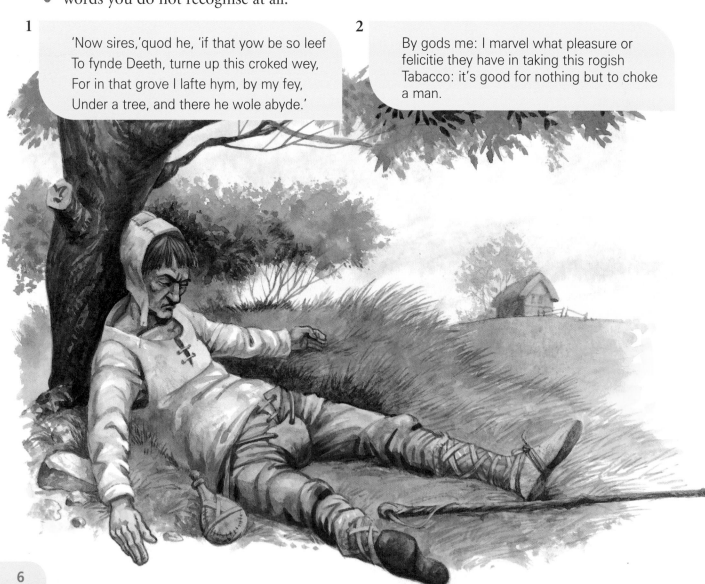

3

Sōthlīce his yldra sunu wæs on æcere; and hē cōm, and tha hē tham hūse genealæhte, hē gehyrde thæne sweg and thæt wered.

4

I'm the only one in London who can swallow a snake. There's nobody else besides me. It requires great courage. In the country there is some
5 places where, when you do it, they swear you are the devil, and won't have it nohow.

5

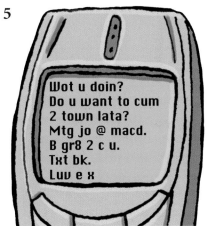

Wot u doin?
Do u want to cum
2 town lata?
Mtg jo @ macd.
B gr8 2 c u.
Txt bk.
Luv e x

3 Now check your answers with your teacher. Work with a partner to discuss the following questions.

a How did you work out the order?

b What have you learnt about:
- the way words have changed
- the way the use of capital letters has changed?

Examining language from the past

You are now going to examine a short extract written by Geoffrey Chaucer in approximately 1380. It is the beginning of a story about three friends and their adventures when they try to capture Death.

Activity 2

1 Work with a partner and try to read the text aloud.

> Thise riotoures thre of whiche I telle,
> Long erst er prime rong of any belle,
> Were set hem in a taverne for to drynke;
> And as they sat they herde a belle clynke
> 5   Biforn a cors, was carried to his grave.

2 List the words you do not recognise in this text.

3 When working out the meaning of a word you do not recognise, it helps to look at the words around it. This is called the context. Use the context of the following words to help you work out their meanings:
- rong
- clynke
- taverne
- cors.

Examining language from the past and the present day

You are now going to examine two texts, one written in the past and one written in the present day. This will help you to recognise the differences and similarities between them by looking closely at the language used by the writers. Both texts are about the sighting of strange creatures.

Strange creatures

Read the extract on the following page by Richard Whitbourne which was written in 1622. He was an explorer and his book is a factual account of his travels. In this extract he describes an encounter with a strange creature. When you have read the extract, answer the questions in Activity 3.

Now also I will not omit to relate something of a strange Creature that I first saw in the yeere 1610, in a morning early as I was standing by the water side, in the Harbour of Saint Johns, which I espied verie swiftly to come swimming towards me, looking cheerefully as it had beene a woman, by the Face, Eyes, Nose, Mouth, Chin, eares, Necke and Forehead:

It seemed to be so beautifull, and in those parts so well proportioned, having round about upon the head, all blew strakes, resembling haire, downe to the Necke (but certainly it was haire) for I beheld it long, and another of my companie also, yet living, that was not then farre from me; and seeing the same comming so swiftly towards mee, I stepped backe, for it was come within the length of a long Pike.

Which when this strange Creature saw that I went from it, it presently thereupon dived a little under water, and did swim to the place where before I landed; whereby I beheld the shoulders and backe downe to the middle, to be as square, white and smooth as the backe of a man, and from the middle to the hinder part, pointing in proportion like a broad hooked Arrow . . .

This I suppose was a mermaid.

From *Discourse and Discovery of Newfoundland* by Richard Whitbourne, 1622

Activity 3

1 What do you notice about:
- the length of the sentences
- the use of capital letters in the first paragraph
- the spelling of words in the second paragraph?

2 Since this is an account of what Richard Whitbourne saw, he has written in the first person, using the pronoun *I*. Because he wants to inform his readers he includes a number of facts about the mermaid.

    a List three facts about the mermaid from Richard Whitbourne's account.

    b At one point he reveals his personal opinion about the creature. What does he say about her?

3 a To help the reader picture the mermaid, the writer uses similes, using the words 'as' and 'like'. Find two similes and write them down.

    b How does each of these similes help to create a picture of the mermaid?

4 This is how the beginning of the third paragraph might be written in modern English:

> When the strange creature saw me step back, it immediately dived a little under the water. Then it swam to where I had been.

Try rewriting the rest of the third paragraph in modern English.

Feedback

Work with a partner. Show them your rewrite of the third paragraph and ask them to check that you have:
- used the modern English spelling of the words
- written in shorter sentences
- adopted the modern use of capital letters.

If you need to, make corrections to your draft.

A monster in the woods

The next text is written in modern standard English. It appeared both on a website and in a magazine.

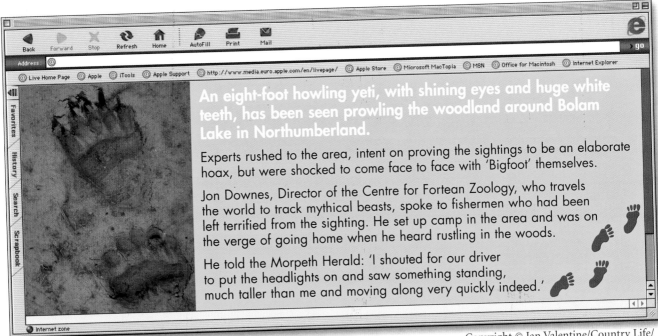

An eight-foot howling yeti, with shining eyes and huge white teeth, has been seen prowling the woodland around Bolam Lake in Northumberland.

Experts rushed to the area, intent on proving the sightings to be an elaborate hoax, but were shocked to come face to face with 'Bigfoot' themselves.

Jon Downes, Director of the Centre for Fortean Zoology, who travels the world to track mythical beasts, spoke to fishermen who had been left terrified from the sighting. He set up camp in the area and was on the verge of going home when he heard rustling in the woods.

He told the Morpeth Herald: 'I shouted for our driver to put the headlights on and saw something standing, much taller than me and moving along very quickly indeed.'

Copyright © Ian Valentine/Country Life/
IPC Syndication

Activity 4

Compare this text with Richard Whitbourne's account on page 9.

1 What do you notice about:
- the length of the sentences
- the use of capital letters?

2 If the following words were used in the modern text, how would they be spelt?
- yeere
- verie
- eares
- Necke
- beautifull
- farre
- comming
- mee

How writers create excitement

The writer uses various techniques to make the sighting of the creature sound dramatic and exciting. He uses:
- **noun phrases** – where a noun has a group of words around it which gives the reader more information about the noun, for example:

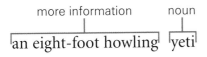

- **association of ideas** – by using words which the reader can associate with something else, the writer can create a dramatic effect, for example:

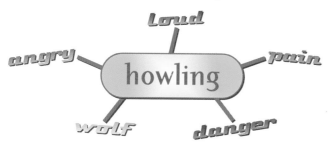

- **direct speech** – by using the actual words of an eyewitness, he makes the event seem more convincing for the reader, for example 'I saw something standing, much taller than me.'

 Activity 5

1 Find and copy another example of a noun phrase in the text. Highlight the noun and the additional information in two different colours.

2 Look at the first two paragraphs of the article and find three more examples of words that the writer uses to make the appearance of the creature seem dramatic and interesting. Write down these words and list other words that readers might associate with them. Set your answers out as spider diagrams – one for each of the three words.

Writing an exciting account

You are now going to use the techniques you have learnt about in your own writing.

 Activity 6

Write an article for a magazine or website about the sighting of an unusual creature. You could use the pictures on page 13 to help you. Aim to make your writing dramatic and exciting. Follow Stages 1–3 on the next page.

 Sharpen spelling

Strategies for learning spellings

Look at the word 'mythical' on line 7 of the website text on page 11. When saying 'mythical' the stress is on the first part of the word, so the ending of the word can be difficult to spell. When the stress is on the first part of the word, your voice often trails off at the end.

When you are learning the spellings of words like this, it is helpful to say the word aloud, stressing the ending so that you can learn to spell it correctly, for example: myth**ic**al

1 Use this method to read these words aloud and learn their spellings.

physic**al**	person**al**
chocol**ate**	priv**ate**
dam**age**	aver**age**
break**able**	suit**able**

2 Can you add at least one more example to each of the four pairs above?

 Highlight thinking

Creative thinking – association
Association means looking at what a word or image suggests – what other things it might be linked to.

This way of thinking is important in English because it can help you to understand how words work in a text to suggest a deeper meaning.

Stage 1

Plan your ideas. Copy the table below and make notes beside each question.

Questions to consider	Notes
When the creature was seen	
What the creature looked like	
How the creature moved	
Who saw the creature	

Stage 2

- List three or four noun phrases you could use to describe your creature.
- Select words to describe your creature that have other associations.
- List two things an eyewitness might say about your creature.

Stage 3

Write your first draft. Follow the structure of the text about the yeti on page 11 by:

- describing the creature
- giving details of where it was seen and by whom
- using direct speech to record the eyewitness's reactions.

 Feedback

Work with a partner.

1 Read your partner's draft and put a tick next to the places where they have used:
   - language that makes the sighting of the creature seem exciting
   - words that have been used to create associations in the reader's mind
   - direct speech of an eyewitness.

2 Write an overall comment explaining:
   - what your partner has done well
   - what your partner could do to improve their work.

3 Write your final draft of the article using your partner's suggestions for improvements.

New words

Language is a living thing. New words are constantly being added to the English language in response to changes in the world around us and the way we think about it.

Activity 7

1 Look at the words below. Some of these words are entirely new and some of them have been made up from words that already exist. Sort out the words by copying and completing the table below.

rollover **chatroom** **blog** **web cam** **bling bling**

scratch card **TEXTING** **cyberslacking** **google** **phat**

Word	Meaning	Is it made up from words that already exist?	What is the connection between the word and it's meaning?
rollover	money carried over from one draw to the next in the lottery	Yes	It connects two ideas of being carried on

2 With a partner, think of at least three other new words. Add them to your table.

Forming new words

New words can also be formed using words which have their origins in other languages. For example, English uses a lot of words taken from Greek or Latin. When the word *television* was introduced to describe a new invention, it was formed from one Greek word and one Latin word: *tele* meaning 'afar' and *vision* meaning 'to see'.

Activity 8

1 The following words all originate in the Greek language. Can you match them with their meanings?

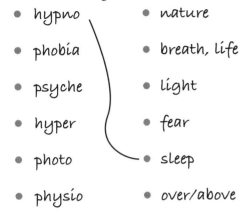

- hypno
- nature
- phobia
- breath, life
- psyche
- light
- hyper
- fear
- photo
- sleep
- physio
- over/above

2 How many words do you know that are formed from the list above? E.g. *hyperactive.*

Sharpen spelling

Learning difficult words

A hypochondriac is a person who is abnormally concerned about his or her health.
It is pronounced like this: <u>hy-po-kon-dree-ak</u>.

At first sight it looks like a tricky word to spell, but if you split it up into syllables and learn the word in small chunks, you will find it much easier to learn – <u>hy/po/chon/dri/ac</u>.
Saying the sounds aloud as you sound out the syllables will help to reinforce your learning.

1 Try the same technique with these words:
- psychiatrist
- agoraphobia
- philosophical.

2 Try the technique with some of the words on the list you made in Activity 7. Work with a partner and test each other.

Standard English, accent and dialect

You will probably have heard the terms standard English, accent and dialect. What do you think they mean?
Check your understanding with the explanations below.

Standard English is the form of English that is most often used in print and is widely understood by all English speakers. Can you think of three situations in which standard English would be used?

Accent refers to the way words are pronounced in different areas. Standard English can be spoken in a wide range of accents.

Dialect is a variety of English, often spoken by people living in a particular area. Dialect has its own vocabulary and use of grammar.

In small groups, talk about:
- when you might use standard English
- different accents you know of
- different dialects you know of.

Activity 9

The spelling in the poem 'Dahn the plug 'ole' shows you the accent of the writer.

1 Read the poem aloud with a partner. Which of these accents does the poem show?

Geordie	Scouse	Cockney
West Indian	Yorkshire	

2 List the spellings that have been adapted to get across the sounds of the words to the reader. Write the standard English spelling next to them.

3 What difference would it have made if the poem had been written in standard English?

 Sharpen punctuation

Semi-colons

We usually separate one sentence from another with a full stop, but sometimes when there is a strong link between two statements the pause between them can be created by using a semi-colon instead.

Semi-colons are used in two places in the poem below. The first one is:

> The biby was gorn; and in anguish she cried,

In this example, the sentence that comes after the semi-colon is linked to the sentence that comes before it – because the baby has gone the mother is upset and cries in anguish.

Find the second example and explain the link between the two sentences.

DAHN THE PLUG 'OLE

A muvver was barfin' 'er biby one night,
The youngest of ten and a tiny young mite,
The muvver was poor and the biby was thin,
Only a skelington covered in skin;
5 The muvver turned rahnd for the soap off the rack,
She was but a moment, but when she turned back,
The biby was gorn; and in anguish she cried,
'Oh where is my biby?'– The angels replied:

'You biby 'as fell dahn the plug-'ole,
10 Your biby 'as gorn dahn the plug;
The poor little thing was so skinny and thin
'E oughter been barfed in a jug.

Anon

Dialect

Differences between standard English and dialect are found in vocabulary and grammar. Here are two activities to help you explore dialect.

Activity 10

1 Look at the examples of dialect vocabulary below.

   a Copy them out and next to each one write one of these letters:

     A = I've never heard this word before.
     B = I've heard this word before but don't know what it means.
     C = I've heard the word and know what it means.

- mard
- bairn
- mither
- dosh
- daps
- bonny
- laking
- chuggy pigs

   b Compare your list with a partner's. If you did not understand all of them, you may find them in a dictionary. Write the standard English word(s) next to the dialect words.

2 With a partner make a list of dialect words that are used for the following terms in the part of the country you come from or from another part of the country that you know.
- bread roll
- happy
- cowardly person
- nothing
- alleyway
- staying away from school deliberately.

Activity 11

Look at this example of dialect speech:

Look at <u>them</u> big spiders!

The use of the word 'them' in this sentence is not standard English grammar. Standard English grammar uses the word 'those', for example:

Look at <u>those</u> big spiders!

1 a Copy the following sentences and underline the part of the sentence which is not standard English grammar.

  b Below each one write the standard English version.

- The film what was on last night was good.
- There was some people here a minute ago.
- She was sat over there.
- I ain't coming.
- We was singing.
- I never broke nothing.
- He done his homework last night.
- You should of left an hour ago.
- I like pasta because it cooks really quick.
- Are you going football tonight?

Activity 12

John Agard is a poet from the Caribbean who now lives and works in England. He often writes poems in dialect.

1 a Read the poem through once, silently.

  b Working with a partner, read the poem aloud. Pronounce the words as they are written.

2 Write the answers to these questions.

  a What history has the poet been taught in school? How does he feel about this?

  b What kind of history would he like to have been taught?

  c Which two lines do you feel best sum up the poet's message? Give reasons for your answer.

  d How would you describe the tone of this poem? Choose two words from this list and explain the reasons for your choice:

- sad
- sarcastic
- bitter
- cheerful
- angry
- proud.

  e In the last line of the poem, John Agard speaks of 'carving out me own identity'.

In what ways do you think the language he uses in this poem helps him to do this?

Checking out me history

Dem tell me
Dem tell me
Wha dem want fo tell me

Bandage up me eye with me own history
5 Blind me to me own identity

Dem tell me bout 1066 and all dat
Dem tell me bout Dick Whittington and he cat
But **Toussaint L'Ouverture**
no dem never tell me bout dat

10 Toussaint
a slave
with vision
lick back
Napoleon
15 battalion
and first Black

Republic born
Toussaint de thorn
to de French
20 Toussaint de beacon
of de Haitian Revolution

Dem tell me bout de man who discover de
   balloon
and de cow who jump over de moon

Dem tell me bout de dish ran away with the
   spoon
but dem never tell me bout **Nanny de maroon**
Nanny
see-far woman
of mountain dream
fire-woman struggle
hopeful stream
to freedom river

Dem tell me bout Lord Nelson and Waterloo
but dem never tell me bout **Shaka de great
   Zulu**
Dem tell me bout Columbus and 1492
35 but what happen to **de Caribs and de
   Arawaks** too

Dem tell me bout Florence Nightingale and
   she lamp
and how Robin Hood used to camp
Dem tell me bout old King Cole was a merry
   old soul
but dem never tell me bout **Mary Seacole**

40 From Jamaica
she travel far
to the Crimean War
she volunteer to go
and even when de British said no
45 she still brave the Russian snow
a healing star
among the wounded
a yellow sunrise
to the dying

50 Dem tell me
Dem tell me wha dem want fo tell me
But now I checking out me own history
I carving out me identity.

John Agard

Word bank

Toussaint L'Ouverture a freed slave who led the fight for
independence in Haiti, an island in the Caribbean, in the 1790s.
lick beat
Nanny de maroon a woman who escaped from slavery and
started a movement to drive the British out of Jamaica
Shaka de great Zulu a famous South African, King of the Zulu
tribe in the 1800s
de Caribs and de Arawaks two tribes, one cannibal and one
peaceful, that lived in the Caribbean in the 1800s
Mary Seacole a pioneering Caribbean nurse and heroine of
the Crimean War

3 Look again at these lines from the poem and read the annotations that show some of the ways in which the dialect of the poem differs from standard English:

Different form of possessive *his*.

Dem tell me bout 1066 and all dat
Dem tell me bout Dick Whittington and he cat
But Toussaint L'Ouverture
No dem never tell me bout dat

Alternative pronunciation of letters shown by use of different consonants: 'd' not 'th'.

Present tense used instead of past tense form of verb.

Sharpen spelling

Apostrophes
Some words are written with an apostrophe. This can indicate that one or more letters have been missed out. The words have been written like this to show the way they would be pronounced.

1 Make a list of the words in Text A on page 21 that are written like this and write the full version next to them, e.g.
You'll ➜ you will

2 Write the shortened form of the following words, using an apostrophe to mark the missing letters: *must not*, *he is*, *they are*.

4 Copy lines 36–9 from the poem and annotate the ways in which the dialect differs from standard English. Look out for:
- alternative pronunciation of letters
- shortened words (e.g. with some letters missing)
- different form of possessive (*his*, *her*, etc.)
- different form of past tense.

Speaking your own language

As you have seen in your work on dialect, the language you use is part of your identity. The language you use when you talk to your friends can be very different from the language you use when you talk to your parents or your teachers.

Slang is the name for informal vocabulary used by a particular group of people. It changes frequently so the slang words your parents used when they were young will be very different from the ones you use today.

Work with a partner to make a list of slang words and phrases you would use for:

good   BIG   happy

BAD   relaxing   money

The texts below are about the same event. Text A is a transcript of a student's informal account of a fire at her school. Text B is a transcript of a formal radio news bulletin which covers the same event. Read both texts closely before doing Activity 13.

Text A

You'll never guess what happened at our school yesterday. There was this ginormous fire in the Science lab. Chazzer said it started in one of those ... y'know .... cupboard things ... y'know like at the side of the room but I didn't see it. Anyways there was smoke all over the place and then the fire alarm went off and Jonesy made us leave everything and just go straight out. She wouldn't even let us put our coats on an' it was freezing outside. She said we could of been burned if we didn't go straight out. Anyways we could see the flames from outside. It was well bad. Mind you, at least Jonesy grabbed the hamsters and the guinea pigs or else they'd of been for it. We had to stay outside for ages while the firemen put the fire out. Anyways the Head's closed the school tomorrow. Wicked!

Text B

A fire broke out earlier today in a Science laboratory at Green Lane High School. The blaze is believed to have been started by an electrical fault.

The alarm was raised by David White, a technician at the school, who was the first to spot the fire. Concerned neighbours hurried to the scene, reporting that flames could be seen from up to two miles away. School staff ensured that all students were evacuated safely. Fortunately animals in the laboratory, two guinea pigs and three hamsters, were also rescued.

The school has been closed until further notice by the Head Teacher, Mrs Thompson, so that the full extent of the damage can be properly assessed.

Activity 13

1 List the details that are in Text A but not Text B. Suggest why these details have been left out of Text B.

2 Write down three examples of slang in Text A.

3 What do you notice about the use of names in the two texts?

4 Text A is written in the first person (*I*, *we*). What person is Text B written in? Can you give a reason for the difference?

5 Text B is written in more formal English. Formal English is more likely to use the passive voice.

When a verb is active the subject performs the action, for example:

When a verb is passive the subject is on the receiving end of the action, for example:

Subject   verb

⌐A fire⌐ ⌐destroyed⌐ the building

Subject   verb

⌐The building⌐ ⌐was destroyed⌐ by fire.

You will notice that in the passive version the verb has changed slightly.

Re-read Text B to find and write down the passive, more formal, form of the following:

- it started
- the fire alarm went off
- we could see the flames
- the Head's closed the school tomorrow.

Activity 14

Read this informal text closely. You are going to rewrite it as a formal news bulletin.

Loads of people in our area have had their bikes stolen but I never in a million years thought it would happen to me. I was doing my paper round, which is a bit of a hassle but it does bring in some cash, when someone pinched it – well, bits of it. I wouldn't mind but I'd locked it up with the bike lock and everything.

I chained it to this lamp-post and went up the path to that house on the corner, the one with the well big garden. When I came back some cheeky so-and-so had pinched the saddle and the front wheel! My mum phoned the police but they didn't seem too hopeful.

Stage 1
- List the facts you will include in the bulletin.
- Make a note of the slang words you need to avoid using.
- Think about how you will change the first person to the third person.
- Make up any names that are needed or helpful.
- Think about how you could replace active verbs with passive verbs.

Stage 2
Look back at Text B on page 21. Use this as a model for your first draft. Aim to write a clear introduction, a more detailed explanation and a clear conclusion.

Stage 3
To help you assess your first draft:
a highlight where you have used:
- formal language instead of slang
- passive verbs.
b highlight in different colours the lines that form your:
- introduction
- detailed explanation
- conclusion.
c read the bulletins of other students in your class.

Stage 4
Make changes and improvements to your first draft before writing your final copy.

 Progress check

Imagine that you have to explain to a Year 7 student how to write a formal news bulletin. Using the bulletin you have just written as an example, make notes on what you would explain about the use of:
- slang
- passive verbs
- standard English
- the third person.

If you have difficulty making notes on what to say, look back to pages 21–2 to help you. You could also work with a partner on anything you or they find difficult.

The power of words

People often use words to attract attention. For example, the owners of shops and businesses use interesting or unusual names to attract customers.

Activity 15

1 Look at these shop names, which all use words to attract attention. What do you think these shops sell or what kind of service do they provide?

2 Some of the shop names above rely on a pun to get readers' attention. A pun is a play on words. It uses words or phrases with similar sounds or spellings but different meanings to create an effect, for example:

Grate Expectations uses the word 'grate' to tell customers they sell fire-places and grates. The word 'expectations' suggests that the shop has high standards and that customers will be satisfied if they shop there. The whole phrase 'Grate Expectations' will remind customers of the title of the novel <u>Great Expectations</u> by Charles Dickens and so will stick in their minds.

a Choose two other names on the list above that rely on puns. Explain the names to a partner.

b Two of the names deliberately use a mis-spelling. Which ones are these? Can you explain why the names have been deliberately mis-spelt?

c The name *Wings and Fins* relies on the sound of the words to get attention. Can you explain why?

3 Devise your own names for:
- a sports shop
- a computer games shop
- a bookshop
- a pet shop.

Activity 16

Paint manufacturers often describe their colours with words that create a mood or a picture, for example:

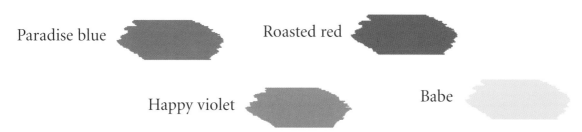

English forest

Paradise blue   Roasted red

Happy violet   Babe

Highlight thinking

Creative thinking: linking ideas

This sort of thinking is creative because you make links between ideas and objects that you might not normally connect. In Activity 15 you have been exploring links suggested by words and puns, e.g. fireplaces and Charles Dickens.

This sort of thinking is useful to writers because it can:
- suggest a lot in a single word or a phrase
- get the reader's attention.

The names above rely on readers making associations with the names of the colours. For example 'roasted red' suggests something which is warm.

1 Look at the other colours and suggest associations for them.

2 Create your own names for the colours below and explain why you have chosen them.

Activity 17

Look at the following page, which is taken from an Easter egg box. You are going to examine how the writer has used the power of words to influence readers. Answer questions 1 to 10 as you read.

1 Why has a noun phrase been used here? Find two other examples of noun phrases in the text and explain the impact on readers of grouping words around a noun.

2 This is an invented word. What words is it based on? What impression does the writer want to create?

6 Why has the writer used this word?

Kandy's

Kaleidostars™

A variety of 5 unbelievable taste sensations

Dark chocolate egg flavoured with real mint with an assortment of chocolates

Dark Kaleidostars™ chocolate studded with chewy golden caramel

The delicious taste of Kaleidostars™ milk chocolate

If you've enjoyed the minty taste of our Kandy's Kaleidostars™ Easter egg, why not treat yourself to a box of Kaleidostars™?

7 How might this phrase make the product appealing to readers?

Milk Kaleidostars™ chocolate wrapped around a whole hazelnut

The perfect way to treat friends and family, or to devour yourself if you don't like sharing!

8 What impression does this word give?

9 Can you make a link between this word and the quality of the chocolate?

A scrumptious star of white Kaleidostars™ chocolate

190 g ℮

Dark Kaleidostars™ chocolate with a naughty mint fondant centre

3 Why do you think this word is used? What impression does it give? Can you think of any other phrase which uses the word 'studded'?

4 What is the key word in this sentence? What impression does this give of the chocolate?

5 Why do you think this word has been used?

10 How do the colours and the designs appeal to customers?

Design a new chocolate bar wrapper

Activity 18

Work in groups to create a new chocolate bar and to design its wrapper. You will present your ideas to another group of students. Follow these stages:

Stage 1

1 In your group, talk about the kind of chocolate bar you want to create. Think about its taste, appearance and texture. Will it be creamy or crunchy? Dark or milk chocolate? What flavour(s) will it have? Will it have a filling? List your decisions.

2 Write two or three noun phrases to describe your chocolate bar. Aim to build up a detailed description of its taste, texture and appearance.

Stage 2

Invent a name. You could base its name on:
- an exotic place
- an animal
- a planet
- something else.

Stage 3

List words and phrases to:
- describe the experience of eating your chocolate bar
- tell readers that eating your chocolate bar will be a very enjoyable experience. Aim to use rhyme or repetition for extra effect.

Stage 4

1 Use these prompts to help you think about the design and layout of your wrapper.
- What pictures or design features will you include?
- In what order will you place the words and phrases?
- Where will you place the words and the pictures?
- What colours will you choose for your wrapper?

2 Now work together to produce your final text and design.

Stage 5

Prepare your presentation. Decide who will say what. Use the checklist below to help you structure your explanation.

- How and why you chose the name for your chocolate bar.
- How you used words to make your chocolate bar sound delicious.
- Which language techniques you used for effect, for example repetition.
- Why you made your choice of pictures and colours.

Some useful words to use in explanations are: *because, for this reason, so that, in order to.*

 Highlight thinking

Critical thinking: evaluating

Evaluation means making a judgement about how effective something is. To evaluate successfully you need to:

- understand and use criteria – what is your judgement based on?
- be prepared to explain your evaluation according to the criteria.

When you evaluate your own and your classmates' work, you use your understanding of what makes a successful piece of English work for the assignment as your criteria. This helps strengthen your understanding, as well as improving your work.

 Feedback

1 Now you are going to present your new chocolate bar to other students. Ask them to listen carefully and comment on whether you have:
   - invented an exciting and tasty new chocolate bar
   - invented a memorable name for your chocolate bar
   - used noun phrases to describe the chocolate bar
   - used language techniques e.g. repetition to make impact
   - presented your ideas clearly.

   The other students should explain their comments and suggest improvements you could make.

2 Use their feedback to help you evaluate your design.
   a Write two or three sentences explaining how successful your design was in making an impact.
   b If you were to do a similar task again, explain what you would do differently and why.

Assessment task

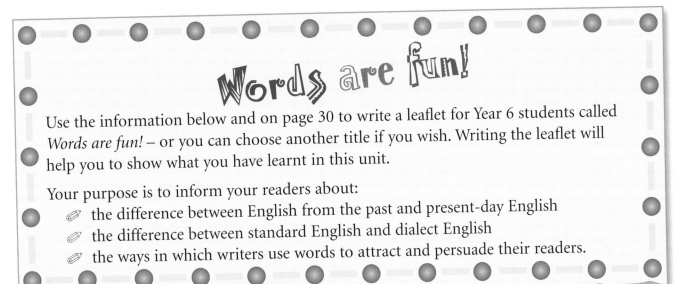

Words are fun!

Use the information below and on page 30 to write a leaflet for Year 6 students called *Words are fun!* – or you can choose another title if you wish. Writing the leaflet will help you to show what you have learnt in this unit.

Your purpose is to inform your readers about:

- the difference between English from the past and present-day English
- the difference between standard English and dialect English
- the ways in which writers use words to attract and persuade their readers.

The success criteria for the task are as follows:

- use clear explanations and language that Year 6 students will understand easily
- organise and present information to make your leaflet attractive, fun and interesting to read
- use a level of formality appropriate to your audience and to the purpose of the leaflet
- give examples of some of the differences between English written in the past and present-day English
- give examples of standard English and dialect English and explain the differences between them clearly
- explain how writers get their readers' attention and persuade them to buy a product
- use extracts from the following six texts as examples, and add your own examples where helpful.

2 September 1666

You were almost burned with a shower of firedrops. We saw the fire as only one entire arch of fire from this to the other side of the bridge. It made me weep to see it. The churches, houses, and all on fire and flaming at once, and a horrid noise the flames made, and the cracking of houses at their ruine.

Adapted from *Samuel Pepys's Diary*

Names of lipsticks

Posh Pink

Cherry Lips

Mad Magenta

Raspberry Ice

Daring Red

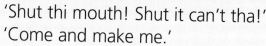

'Shut thi mouth! Shut it can't tha!'
'Come and make me.'
'Tha can only pick on little kids. Tha daren't pick on anybody thi own size!'
'Who daren't?'
'Thee! Tha wouldn't say what tha's just said to our Jud. He'd murder thi.'
'I'm not frightened of him.'
'Tha would be if he wa' here.'
'Would I heck, he's nowt, your Jud.'

From A *Kestrel for a Knave* by Barry Hines

Doctor, can you make my spots go away?
I'm afraid I can't make any rash promises.

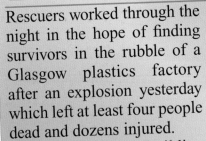

Rescuers worked through the night in the hope of finding survivors in the rubble of a Glasgow plastics factory after an explosion yesterday which left at least four people dead and dozens injured.

The four-storey building collapsed instantly. Outside, people could not believe what they were seeing. Inside, there was only darkness and panic as debris and dust consumed the scene.

Daniel Gilmour was on the ground floor. 'It just went pitch black with all the dust and I didn't know if there was anyone there so I shouted to my mate Jimmy,' he said, blood dripping from head injuries.

From the *Guardian*

Forsoth his eldere sone was in the feeld, and whanne he cam and neighede to the houe, he herde a symfonye and a croude. And he clepide oon of the seruauntis, and axide what thingis thes weren.

The Bible, 1380

Getting started

1 List your ideas under these headings:

Introduction

Explain to your Year 6 readers what the purpose of the leaflet is and what they can expect to find in it.

How English has changed
- texts I will use
- differences I will point out
- my opening sentence
- presentational features I will use.

Differences between standard English and dialect English
- texts I will use
- what I want my readers to know
- how I will begin my explanation
- presentational features I will use.

Attracting and persuading readers
- texts I will use
- order in which I will write about the various techniques
- presentational features I will use.

2 When you have made your notes and selected your texts, write your first draft. If you want to include pictures, do a rough sketch only at this stage. While you are writing, keep checking the success criteria on page 29.

3 Show your first draft to another student. Ask them to check that you have included everything in the success criteria. They should tick the places in your text where you have met the criteria and annotate your text with suggestions for improvement.

4 Use your partner's suggestions to help you write your final draft.

5 When you have finished writing, evaluate your leaflet.

  a Read through your completed leaflet again and award yourself one, two or three stars for each of the features on the success criteria list on page 29.

   One star = I could have done this better.

   Two stars = I think I did this well, but I could make one or two improvements.

   Three stars = I did this really well.

  b Now copy and complete this sentence:

   If I were to write another leaflet like this one, I would . . .

2 Crafting writing

The bigger picture

In this unit you will explore how writers use a variety of forms and techniques to engage readers. You will discover how writers develop key ideas in different ways by reading texts, including travel writing, a short story and a poem. At the end of the unit you will create your own piece of writing, using the techniques you have explored.

WHAT? You will:
- explore how similar themes can be written about in different ways and forms
- consider the ways writers structure their writing and the techniques they use to engage the reader
- develop your ability to use a range of techniques in your own writing

HOW? by:
- reading a range of texts and examining how they are organised
- studying how writers use tone, figurative language, suspense and repetition to engage the reader
- writing your own texts modelled on what you have read

WHY? because:
- by reading a range of writing on similar themes you can begin to appreciate the approaches you could take in your own writing
- by exploring the ways real writers work, you will able to apply what you have learned to your own writing.

Choices writers make

How a writer chooses to write about something depends on:
- the purpose of the writing
- the kind of reader the writing is aimed at.

Activity 1

Read the following short extracts about different places and then answer the questions. Note down how you worked out your answers.

1 Is the writing fiction, non-fiction or poetry? Explain how you know this.

2 Where might you find this kind of writing? Choose from the following:

- travel guide
- anthology of poetry
- dictionary
- letter
- encyclopedia
- novel
- magazine
- website

For each text, explain your choice.

A

Costs, Money and Banks

Most basic items in Canada cost less than in Britain and a bit more than they do in the US; more specific details are given below and throughout the Guide. Generally, if
5 you're sticking to a very tight budget – camping and buying food from shops – you could squeeze through on £25/US$40/C$60 a day. You're not going to last long living like this, though, and a more comfortable
10 average daily budget, covering a motel room, bus travel, a museum or two and a restaurant meal would work out at around £65/US$100/C$150.

B

A faint streak in the E., gradually paling the brightness of the stars, heralds the birth of day. This insensibly changes to a band of gold
5 on the horizon; each lofty peak becomes tinged with a roseate blush; the shadows between the Rigi and the horizon melt away; forests, lakes, hills, towns, and
10 villages are revealed; all is grey and cold, until the sun bursts from behind the mountains in all his majesty, flooding the superb landscape with light and warmth.

C

He scattered tarantulas over the roads,
Put thorns on the cactus and horns on the toads,
He sprinkled the sands with millions of ants
So the man who sits down must wear soles on his pants.
5 He lengthened the horns of the Texas steer,
And added an inch to the jack rabbit's ear;
He put mouths full of teeth in all of the lakes,
And under the rocks he put rattlesnakes.

D

> It began on a winter's evening, when the townsfolk were gathering in the White Horse Tavern. The snow was blowing down from the mountains, and the wind was making the bells shift restlessly in the church tower. The windows were steamed up, the stove was blazing brightly, Putzi, the old
> 5 black cat, was snoozing on the hearth; and the air was full of the rich smells of sausage and sauerkraut, of tobacco and beer. Gretl, the little barmaid, the landlord's daughter, was hurrying to and fro with foaming mugs and steaming plates.

E

DANUBE

> Great south-eastward-flowing river of Europe, 1,750 miles long. Rises in Black Forest, Germany, winds through highlands of Germany, Austria, across plains of Hungary and Rumania, until reaching Black Sea in delta.

Activity 2

One significant difference between texts can be the way the writer chooses to use facts and opinions. A fact can be proved to be true. An opinion cannot be proved to be true or false; it is a point of view. Being able to identify facts and opinions is especially important when reading travel writing, as a reader might want to visit the place being described.

1 Read the following two sections from the extracts and decide which one expresses an opinion.
   a List the words or phrases which support your ideas.
   b Explain the writer's purpose in each case.

> all is grey and cold, until the sun bursts from behind the mountains in all his majesty, flooding the superb landscape with light and warmth. (Text B)

> Rises in Black Forest, Germany, winds through highlands of Germany, Austria, across plains of Hungary and Rumania. (Text E)

2 Now read the following section from Text A:

> Generally, if you're sticking to a very tight budget – camping and buying food from shops – you could squeeze through on £25/US$40/C$60 a day.

   a Is the writer expressing an opinion or stating facts?
   b The writer begins with 'if you're …' and continues with 'you could'.
   Is the writer:
   - stating a fact with absolute certainty?
   - stating a strong possibility?
   - expressing a vague possibility?

   c How would the meaning of the sentence be changed if *could* was replaced by each of the words *will*, *might*, *should*? Decide whether the writer's view would be expressed more strongly or with more doubt.

Activity 3

Although Text C, which is a poem about Texas, is not a non-fiction text, it does contain a number of facts. For example, it states that there are deserts and cactus plants in Texas.

1 List five other facts about Texas from the poem.

2 Text E is from an encyclopedia. It uses a heading, is short, factual and written in the present tense. Using the facts from the poem, write a short text about Texas in the style of an encyclopedia entry. Give your text a heading, be factual and write in the present tense.

Activity 4

Modal verbs allow the writer to suggest the likelihood of events. There are ten modal verbs: *can, could, may, might, will, would, shall, should, ought, must.* When you want to express an opinion, these verbs and the differences between them help the reader to understand the strength of your feeling.

Highlight thinking

Creative thinking: considering alternatives

Considering alternatives means thinking of another way of doing or saying or looking at something. This can help you to think through problems, or to understand why someone else has made the choices they have made.

A useful way of exploring language and understanding the ways words work is to replace the writer's word or phrase with another. Thinking about how the meaning has changed helps you understand why the writer chose the original words, and what effect they have on the reader.

You will also be using this technique later in the unit, in Activity 7.

Write out the following sentence three times, filling in the gap with a different modal verb each time. First, use a verb which suggests the strongest likelihood of the event, then work your way down to the least likely.

I _____ stay in tonight to do my homework.

✓ Progress check

So far in this unit you have learnt to:
- identify facts and opinions
- understand how modal verbs can be used to suggest different strengths of feeling.

You are going to produce an A4 poster that could be used as a quick reference guide on facts and opinions for other Year 8 students. You should explain the difference between a fact and an opinion, and give an example of a statement that includes one fact and one opinion. You could use examples from Texts 1–5 on pages 33–4 to make your explanations as clear as possible. Your finished poster will show how well you understand facts and opinions.

Following the development of a writer's ideas

Writers will have different **purposes** when they write. Sometimes their main purpose is to express a personal point of view.

Read the newspaper article below, in which the writer expresses her opinion about the reputation of French waiters for being rude. The activities that follow will help you explore the writer's ideas and the ways she structures them.

Service with a snarl

Travel View by Escape Editor Jeanette Hyde

Oh no, it's that time of year again when French tourism chiefs get stroppy waiters and shopkeepers to sign contracts saying they'll smile more and be nicer to foreigners. This year's marketing slogan is: 'In France the smile comes from the heart.'

In what's officially known as the *Bonjour* campaign – now in its eighth year – hoteliers, restaurateurs and visitor attractions are being asked to make a commitment to good service and get away from the offhand and aloof reputation plaguing the country.

But why bother?

Every time you go to France, there's no avoiding the 'service with a snarl' syndrome. At Toulouse airport last year, I ordered a Diet Coke in my worst GCSE French. The Coke that arrived was a sugar-laden normal one and I asked the waiter to change it for a low-cal variety.

The waiter told me it was Diet Coke and that I was completely mistaken. Eventually after much hand-waving and arguing he conceded that it wasn't Diet Coke and 'it was the machine's fault'. He refused to change it, charged the full whack and added a hefty service charge.

When I told an English friend who lives in France about the experience she said British people get stroppy service because they don't know how to communicate with the French. 'It irritates them the way you don't try to speak French. If you don't say *merci* followed by a *Monsieur* you are being rude, and if you say *tu* instead of *vous* they won't come back to your table.'

I probably failed on all three counts. Which made me wonder: shouldn't the French tourism chiefs stop this corny smiling-from-the-heart marketing nonsense?

If we want good service, shouldn't we just make a bit more effort on the language front? Dust down the phrasebook and buy a pocket dictionary?

Exploring how the writer organises ideas

This is how the writer presents her ideas:

A She introduces the topic – the seeming rudeness of French waiters and shopkeepers.

B She tells a story which illustrates the kind of thing she is writing about.

C She provides an explanation for the rudeness of French waiters.

D She states her opinion and suggests a solution.

Activity 5

1 Match the eight paragraphs of the article to the four stages, A–D. Copy and complete the chart below:

Stage	Paragraphs
A	
B	
C	
D	

2 Now look in more detail at the paragraphs in the newspaper article.

- Paragraph 3 is quite unusual because it is so short. Why do you think the writer chose to make this short sentence a separate paragraph, rather than add it to the end of the second paragraph?
- When the writer tells her story about being served by a French waiter, she breaks it down into two paragraphs, 4 and 5. Explain why she organised it like this, rather than simply writing it in one paragraph.

3 Writers link paragraphs so that readers can follow the sequence of their ideas. The first sentence of a new paragraph should connect in some way with what was in the previous paragraph. For example, paragraph 5 begins 'The waiter told me …' This obviously connects with 'I asked the waiter …' in the last sentence of paragraph 4 as the writer continues the story.

Look at the opening sentences of paragraphs 6 and 7 and write a brief explanation of how each one connects with the previous paragraph.

 Sharpen punctuation

Hyphens

The writer of the article on page 36 uses hyphens in two ways:

Hyphens

1 To make an adjective before a noun by joining two words together:

> sugar-laden normal one

2 To invent new adjectives which are a combination of words.

> smiling-from-the-heart marketing nonsense

Create some joined-up adjectives of your own, using hyphens, which could be used in the following sentences:

a She looked at her mother with those _____ eyes.

b He was driving one of those _____ cars.

c She spoke into her _____ mobile phone.

4 The final three sentences could have been written in the following ways:

- … the French tourism chiefs should stop this corny smiling-from-the-heart marketing nonsense.
- If we want good service, we should just make a bit more effort on the language front.
- Dust down the phrasebook and buy a pocket dictionary.

Why do you think the writer chose to write them as questions?

Organising your own writing

You can use these four simple steps to organise your own writing to express an opinion:

Step 1: Introduce a topic.

For example: Where I live there is nothing for young people to do so that …

Step 2: Tell a brief story which illustrates the problem.

For example: Because young people are hanging around on the street corner there has been some trouble …

Step 3: Add some more information.

For example: This led to …

Step 4: State your own opinion about what should be done.

For example: I think …

Activity 6

Write your own text expressing your opinion. Use the topic above or choose a different topic. When you write, follow the steps above and use the features you explored in *Service with a snarl*:

- short paragraphs with no more than three sentences in a paragraph
- a very short one-sentence paragraph to highlight the issue you are writing about
- paragraphs clearly linked with the previous one
- statements turned into questions, as used by the writer at the end of the article.

Feedback

When you have finished, show your writing to a partner. When you read your partner's text, check that:

- their writing has been organised into short paragraphs
- the paragraphs link with each other
- they have used a short one-sentence paragraph effectively
- they successfully use question marks to turn statements into questions.

If they have not included all of these features, highlight which ones are missing and suggest how they could be included.

✓ Progress check

When you have received feedback, grade the following:

- I can organise short pieces of writing helpfully into paragraphs.
- I can link paragraphs so that my writing flows from one point to the next.
- I can use very short paragraphs for effect.

 I need to spend more time looking at these things.

I have done these things fairly well, but there are one or two places where I could have done more.

I have done this well.

Establishing the tone of a piece of writing

Writers establish a tone when they write, which may be humorous, serious, angry or many other tones.

Activity 7

1 Look back at *Service with a snarl* on page 36. The writer criticises rude French waiters but she also seems to criticise English people who can't be bothered to learn and use some French words and phrases. How would you describe the tone of the writing?

Consider the following possible answers:
- It is a very angry piece of writing.
- She is gently mocking.
- She is very sarcastic.
- She is being comic.

2 Read the extract on the next page in which the writer Redmond O'Hanlon is travelling in Borneo with his colleague, James Fenton, who is a poet. As you read it, look at the annotations which draw your attention to the **tone** of the writing and ask you some questions.

Into the Heart of Borneo

It was time to go to bed. We washed our mess-tins in the river, kicked out the fire on the beach, and stoked up the smoking-house fire with more wet logs. Slinging my soaking clothes from a tree with parachute cord, I rubbed
5 myself down with a wet towel and, naked, opened my **Bergen** to pull out my set of dry kit for the night. Every nook and cranny in the bag was alive with inch-long ants. Deciding that anything so huge must be the Elephant ant, and not the Fire ant, which packs a sting like a wasp, I
10 brushed the first wave off my y-fronts. Glancing up, I was astonished to see my wet clothes swarming with ants, too; a procession of dark ants poured down one side of the rope and up the other, and, all over my wet trousers, hundreds of different moths were feeding. Darkness
15 seemed to rise from the leafy mush of the forest floor; and I rummaged quickly in the outside Bergen pocket for my army torch. As my fingers closed on it, everyone else's little fingers seemed to close on my arm. I drew it out fast and switched on: Elephant ants, this time with massive
20 pincers, were suspended from hand to elbow. The soldiers had arrived. I flicked them off, gratified to hear yelps from James's **basha** as I did so. It was good to know they also went for poets.

by Redmond O'Hanlon

If the writer had wanted to create a serious, scary tone how could he have phrased this differently?

This word does not make the ants seem very dangerous or frightening. What phrase could make them seem so?

What phrase could make the ants seem more unpleasant than 'flicked them off'?

What does the final sentence reveal about the writer's feelings about the whole incident?

Word bank

Bergen a kind of back-pack
basha a tent

3 The writer's choice of words creates the tone. So by choosing different words a writer can change the tone. Read the following changes to the original text and describe how the changes affect the tone of the writing:

> *Original:* As my fingers closed on it, everyone else's little fingers seemed to close on my arm. I drew it out fast and switched on.
>
> *Changed version:* As my fingers tentatively closed on it, everyone else's claws seemed to pierce my unprotected arm. I desperately pulled it out fast and nervously switched on.

4 Copy the following sentence from the extract and adapt it to make the tone more frightened or disgusted. Change the underlined words and add new words or phrases in the gaps.

> Glancing up, I was astonished to see my wet clothes swarming with _____ ants, too; a procession of dark ants poured down one side of the rope and up the other, and, all over my wet trousers, hundreds of different _____ moths were feeding.

Feedback

When you have written your version of the sentence, show it to a partner. Your partner should give you some brief written feedback, for example:

'I think you have changed the tone and made the writing seem ...'

'The most effective change you have made is where you have ...'

Writing to entertain

Travel writers, like Redmond O'Hanlon, the author of *Into the Heart of Borneo*, often use a great deal of description to write about the places they visit on their travels. They craft the language they use very carefully to entertain their readers.

Read the next section of *Into the Heart of Borneo* below, then answer the questions that follow. The writer tells a simple story about trying to go to sleep in the jungle while different animals and insects make noises outside his tent. As you read, focus on the way the writer uses description. What kind of tone does he create in the way he chooses to describe things?

Slipping under the mosquito net, I fastened myself into
25 the dark-green camouflage SAS tube. It seemed
luxuriously comfortable. You had to sleep
straight out like a rifle; but the ants, swarming
along the poles, rearing up on their back legs
to look for an entry, and the mosquitoes,
30 whining and singing outside the various
tunes of their species in black shifting
clouds, could not get in.

'Eeeeeee – ai – yack yack yack yack
yack!' Something screamed in my ear,
35 with brain-shredding force. And then
everyone joined in.

'Eeeeeee – ai – yack yack yack yack
yack te yooo!' answered every other
giant male **cicada**, manically vibrating
40 the **tymbals**, drumskin membranes in
their cavity amplifiers, the megaphones
built into their bodies.

'Shut up!' I shouted.

'Wah Wah Wah Wah Wah!' said four thousand
45 frogs.

'Stop it at once!' yelled James.

'Clatter clitter clatter' went our **mess-tins** over the shingle,
being nosed clean by tree shrews.

The **Iban** laughed. The river grew louder in the darkness. Something hooted.
50 Something screamed in earnest further off. Something shuffled and snuffled
around the discarded rice and fish bits flung in a bush from our plates. A
porcupine? A **civet**? A ground squirrel? The long-tailed giant rat? Why not a
Clouded leopard? Or, the only really dangerous mammal in Borneo, the long-
clawed, short-tempered Sun bear?

55 I switched off the torch and tried to sleep. But it was no good.
The decibel-level was way over the limit allowed in discotheques.
And, besides, the fire-flies kept flicking their own torches on and off; and
some kind of phosphorescent fungus glowed in the dark like a forty-watt bulb.

Word bank

Iban the name of a tribe of people in Borneo
cicada an insect, like a grasshopper
civet a small animal, like a cat
tymbals drums
mess-tins metal bowls for food

Activity 8

1 One way writers achieve their effect is to use **metaphors**. Metaphors describe something as if it were something else. For example, in the first paragraph the writer describes mosquitoes as if they were human beings 'whining and singing'.

Highlight thinking

Creative thinking: using the senses
Using your senses is a useful tool for you when you write. You can make your writing more real and vivid if you try to involve all the senses: sound, smell, touch and taste as well as vision.

a Find at least two other instances in the text where the writer uses words that describe animals or insects as if they were human beings.

b Do you agree or disagree with these statements about the possible effects of describing the animals in this way?
  - It makes fairly boring creatures seem more interesting.
  - It makes the creatures seem less threatening.
  - It makes the writing humorous.

2 To make the description entertaining, the writer attempts to capture the sounds made. For example, he writes 'Eeeeeee – ai – yack yack yack yack yack!' instead of simply writing something like 'The cicadas shrieked in my ear'.

a Write five or six sentences of your own in which you aim to entertain your readers by describing animal or insect noises. Your tone should be comic rather than serious. Use the same two methods as the writer.
  - Describe the animals/insects as if they were human.
  - Try to capture the sounds they make.

You could use the ideas below or think of your own.
  - The sound of a bluebottle buzzing around a room.
  - Two cats meeting in the night.

You should only write five or six sentences and have a clear focus on trying to entertain the reader by using the two techniques.

Feedback

Work with a partner.
  1 Read your sentences aloud so that your partner can hear the sounds you are describing.

  2 Explain the ways in which your animal or insect is like a human being. You could begin: 'I'm trying to make it sound as though . . .'

Exploring the structure of a text

You are now going to read a complete short story and focus on how a writer structures a piece of writing.

At the beginning of a short story a writer will often:
- set the scene
- introduce the main characters
- draw readers in by setting up a problem that needs to be resolved.

Activity 9

1 Read the sentence below which opens the short story, *The Gift*:

> Tomorrow would be Christmas and even while the three of them rode to the rocket port, the mother and father were worried.

2 A lot of information is packed into one sentence.
   a What do you know about the time and place in which the story is set?
   b Which characters are mentioned?
   c What situation is set up so that the reader wants to know more ?

You can use the sentence as a model for writing your own intriguing opening sentences to short stories, for example:

A setting is established.   A character is introduced.

> Today was his first day at his new school and as Sean cycled into the grounds, he wondered if today would be any better than the last two.

A problem is set up.

3 Write three different opening sentences for three different short stories, using the model above. Make sure you establish a setting, introduce a character and set up a problem. Use the short-story types below or choose your own:
- a horror story
- a love story
- a science fiction story.

Activity 10

You are going to read the whole story. As you read, answer the questions between the sections of the story.

First, read the rest of the opening section to see how the 'problem' created by the writer is developed.

THE GIFT

Tomorrow would be Christmas and even while the three of them rode to the rocket port, the mother and father were worried. It was the boy's first flight into space, his very first time in a rocket, and they wanted everything to be perfect. So when, at the customs table, they were forced to leave behind his gift which exceeded the weight limit by no more than a few ounces and the little tree with the lovely white candles, they felt themselves deprived of the season and their love.

5

The boy was waiting for them in the Terminal room. Walking towards him, after their unsuccessful clash with the Interplanetary officials, the mother and father whispered to each other.

10 'What shall we do?'

'Nothing, nothing. What *can* we do?'

'Silly rules!'

'And he so wanted the tree!'

The siren gave a great howl and people pressed forward into the Mars Rocket.

15 The mother and father walked at the very last, their small pale son between them, silent.

'I'll think of something,' said the father.

'What … ?' asked the boy.

And the rocket took off and they were flung headlong into dark space.

1 What is the problem – the cause of the parents' worry – that needs to be resolved in the story?

2 The argument between the parents and the Interplanetary officials is just mentioned, no details are given. Why do you think the writer chose to leave out the details ?

3 Science fiction stories can often be recognised because the story focuses on things such as technology, space travel and aliens. In this story, the writer doesn't seem so interested in technology as he gives very little description of the rocket or the take-off. There is much more description of the jungle in Borneo (pages 40 and 42), where the writer chose to focus on details of the setting rather than characters or story. What does this tell you about his purpose in writing the text?

4 In the opening section of *The Gift*, the writer had the opportunity to describe the setting of the Terminal building and the spacecraft in great detail, but chose not to. What other aspects of the story did he choose to focus on?

Now read the middle section of the story. In this section the problem becomes more complicated.

DEPARTURES
PADS 1-4

20   The rocket moved and left fire behind and left Earth behind on which the date was 24 December 2052, heading out into a place where there was no time at all, no month, no year, no hour. They slept away the rest of the first 'day'. Near midnight, by their Earth-time New York watches, the boy awoke and said, 'I want to go look out the porthole.'

25   There was only one port, a 'window' of immensely thick glass, of some size, up on the next deck.

'Not quite yet,' said the father. 'I'll take you up later.'

'I want to see where we are and where we're going.'

'I want you to wait, for a reason,' said the father.

30   He had been lying awake, turning this way and that, thinking of the abandoned gift, the problem of the season, the lost tree and the white candles. And at last, sitting up, no more than five minutes ago, he believed he had found a plan. He need only carry it out and this journey would be fine and joyous indeed.

'Son,' he said, 'in exactly one half-hour it will be Christmas.'

35   'Oh,' said the mother, dismayed that he had mentioned it. Somehow she had rather hoped the boy would forget.

The boy's face grew feverish and his lips trembled. 'I know, I know. Will I get a present, will I? Will I have a tree? You promised –'

'Yes, yes, all that, and more,' said the father.

40   The mother started. 'But – '

'I mean it,' said the father. 'I really mean it. All and more, much more. Excuse me, now. I'll be back.'

5   What makes the problem more difficult or complicated in this section?

6   The writer uses the characters of the mother and father to create tension. What is the difference between their attitudes towards finding a suitable way to celebrate Christmas?

7   At what stage of this section does the writer hint that the father has resolved the problem of the son's present?

8   There is only a little more of the story to come. Opposite are three predictions **a–c** about what might happen next. Working with a partner, think about the way the writer has presented the story so far and decide what you think about each prediction. Choose from the following responses, focusing on the clues in the text that make you think this:

- It's very improbable.
- It's not likely.
- It's possible.

Write a few sentences to support your answer.

   a I think the father is going to arrange for the boy to fly the rocket. I think this because the story says the father has a plan and that makes it sound as though he might have been planning with someone like the pilot.

   b I think the father is going to give his son some kind of Martian creature as a Christmas present. I think this because the story says they are going to Mars and this might not be the rocket's first journey.

   c I think the father is going to give his son a ray gun for a present because he'll need one on Mars.

9 Make two predictions of your own about what might happen next. Support your predictions with evidence from the text.

Now read the final section of the story.

He left them for about twenty minutes. When he came back he was smiling. 'Almost time.'

45 'Can I hold your watch?' asked the boy, and the watch was handed over and he held it ticking in his fingers as the rest of the hour drifted by in fire and silence and unfelt motion.

   'It's Christmas *now*! Christmas! Where's my present?'

   'Here we go,' said the father, and took his boy by the shoulder and led him 50 from the room, down the hall, up a ramp-way, his wife following.

   'I don't understand,' she kept saying.

   'You will. Here we are,' said the father.

   They had stopped at the closed door of a large room. The father tapped three times and then twice, in a code. The door opened and the light in the cabin 55 went out and there was a whisper of voices.

   'Go on in, son,' said the father.

   'It's dark.'

   'I'll hold your hand. Come on, mama.'

   They stepped into the room and the door shut, and the room was very dark 60 indeed. And before them loomed a great glass eye, the porthole, a window four feet high and six feet wide, from which they could look out into space.

   The boy gasped.

   Behind him, the father and the mother gasped with him, and then in the dark room some people began to sing.

65 'Merry Christmas, son,' said the father.

And the voices in the room sang the old, the familiar carols, and the boy moved forward slowly until his face was pressed against the cool glass of the port. And he stood there for a long long time, just looking and looking out into space and the deep night at the burning and the burning of ten billion billion
70 white and lovely candles. . .

10 Throughout the story the writer has focused on the family of the father, mother and son, and on the problem of what would be an appropriate Christmas present. With a partner, look at the following statements about the writer's main ideas in the story. Note down evidence for each statement from the text. Discuss which ideas you think the writer is making you consider.
   a The writer is mainly interested in the idea of space travel; he likes to describe the rocket and the journey to Mars.
   b This is a story about the father's fight with the Interplanetary officials. Although they take the son's present, the father outwits them.
   c The writer is trying to show what really matters – nature is more important than things like traditional Christmas presents.
   d The writer is showing that the idea of family is very important.

11 Now write down your own thoughts about the writer's main ideas.

The Gift by Ray Bradbury

Exploring the writer's techniques

Creating suspense

Suspense is when the writer keeps readers waiting for important information. In the opening section of the story (page 45), the space-travel setting is established and the three main characters are introduced. The problem is set up – the boy's Christmas present is taken from the family and the parents do not know what to do. But the father says: 'I'll think of something'. From this point on, the reader knows what the problem is and wants to know how it will be resolved.

Activity 11

1 In the middle section of the story (page 46), the writer
- delays the resolution of the problem
- creates suspense.

Explain how the writer does this.

2 At the climax of the story, when the boy is taken to the porthole, the writer again delays the resolution of the problem. Read the ending of the story again, from line 59.
- **a** In this section, before the final sentence, how does the writer show the reader that there is something amazing in the view from the porthole?
- **b** Why does the writer choose to end the story with the word 'candles' rather than 'stars'?

Using repetition

In the last seven sentences of the story, the writer uses a lot of repetition of nouns and connectives.

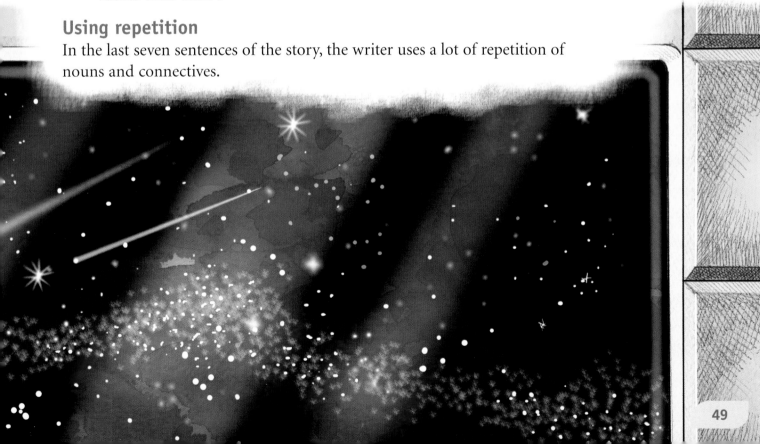

Activity 12

The writer uses the nouns 'father', 'mother' and 'boy', as well as 'son' and 'mama' frequently. Why do you think he uses these words so often? Discuss the following reasons and decide which one is most appropriate:

1 These words constantly remind us that they are a family and that Christmas is a time for families.

2 He doesn't give the characters names because he is not really interested in developing them as characters.

3 It adds some mystery to the story because you don't know very much about the background of the characters.

Activity 13

The writer uses the connective 'and' frequently, sometimes at the start of sentences. However, it isn't always necessary. For example, the final paragraph could be written:

> The voices in the room sang the old, the familiar carols. The boy moved forward slowly until his face was pressed against the cool glass of the port. He stood there for a long long time, just looking out into space and the deep night at the burning of ten billion billion white, lovely candles.

1 With a partner, discuss the following reasons the writer may have chosen to use 'and' so often. Write down the explanation you and your partner prefer.
   a It's a simple tale so he is using simple words.
   b 'And' means 'in addition to' so he's adding details, building up the beauty of the moment.
   c He's trying to show how one thing followed another in a simple way.

2 Using the word 'and' to connect clauses leads the writer to produce quite long sentences. Why do you think he chose to include a very short sentence: 'The boy gasped' and put it as a paragraph on its own?

Writing your own ending

The Gift ends with a scene in which the writer builds up suspense by keeping the reader waiting. Read the last few sentences of the story again, from 'They stepped into the room' (lines 59–70) and work out how the writer builds up the suspense. Now use the ending of this short story as a model for writing your own story ending.

Activity 14

Write a description of some characters entering a room. Just as in *The Gift*, they see something. It might be:

- horrible
- beautiful
- completely unexpected.

Write your description, following the same style as *The Gift*.

- Avoid using names.
- Use 'and' to build up details, and use it at the start of sentences.
- Use repetition of nouns and connectives.
- Use very little dialogue – no more than one line in your whole piece of writing.
- Include a one-sentence paragraph.
- Delay one very important detail until the very end of the story, just as the writer of *The Gift* delayed the detail about the 'candles'.

You could use the original story as a template:

- They stepped into the room ... And before them ... *Describe what they see*
- *Write a one-sentence paragraph*
- Behind ... *describe what is behind them*
- *Write a line of dialogue*
- And ... *Write a conclusion to the incident.*

Aim to write about 135 words (the same length as the ending in *The Gift*) or less.

Feedback

1 When you have finished, read what you have written and comment on:
   - what you have done to introduce some suspense in the writing, by, for example, delaying a very important piece of information
   - whether you feel you have used 'and' successfully
   - how successfully you feel you have organised the writing into paragraphs.
2 Exchange your piece of writing and comments with a partner. Write a brief response to your partner's comments, and say how successfully you think they have achieved the aims.

Using figurative language in poetry

We have already looked at some examples of figurative language in Activity 8 on page 43, when we explored the writer's use of metaphors in *Into the Heart of Borneo*.

Another example of the use of metaphors comes at the end of *The Gift* when the writer is describing the beauty and wonder of the stars:

'the burning of ten billion billion white and lovely candles.' (lines 69–70)

Stars are described as though they are candles.

Poets often use more figurative language than writers of prose. Like *The Gift*, the following poem is about the stars, but the writer uses the verse form to compress a number of ideas about stars into a short piece of writing.

Activity 15

Read the poem below and answer the questions on page 53.

1 In the first two stanzas, how does the writer use metaphors to make stars and planets seem special?

2 Choose one of the metaphors from the first two stanzas which seems especially effective. Explain why you think it works well.

3 In the third stanza, which metaphors show that the earth is different?

Stars and Planets

Trees are cages for them: water holds its breath
To balance them without smudging on its delicate **meniscus**.
Children watch them playing in their heavenly playground;
Men use them to **lug** ships across oceans, through **firths**.

5 They seem so twinkle-still, but they never cease
Inventing new spaces and huge explosions
And migrating in mathematical tribes over
The **steppes** of space at their outrageous ease.

It's hard to think that the earth is one –
10 This poor sad bearer of wars and disasters
Rolls-Roycing round the sun with its load of gangsters,
Attended only by the loveless moon.

Norman MacCaig

Word bank

meniscus the tight surface of water
lug slang for 'pull'
firths narrow inlets of sea into the land
steppes large grassy plains

Using your own metaphors

In 'Stars and Planets', the poet has used metaphors to describe part of the natural world. Now use metaphors to write your own short poem about the natural world.

Activity 16

1 Clouds are an everyday feature of the sky, just like stars. Make a short list of literal things you can say about clouds. Think about:
   ● their appearance
   ● their colour
   ● the way they move
   ● the different kinds of clouds.

   For example:
   Sometimes clouds cover the entire sky.
   They move across the sky.

2 Experiment with ways of describing these literal things in a more imaginative way. For example:

   (literal) They move across the sky.
   (imaginative) They ghost effortlessly across the sky.

   The word 'ghost' has been used to suggest how silently the clouds move and perhaps how they are often white like a ghostly figure.

3 Use your ideas to write a short poem with the title 'Clouds'. Use at least three different metaphors. You might choose to:
   ● describe the variety of clouds
   ● try to get readers to think about ordinary clouds in a way that makes them seem special.

Assessment task

Snappy writing

This task will assess your understanding of the ways a writer uses description and creates tone in a piece of writing. You will then produce a piece of writing of your own, describing one aspect of a place you know.

Read the following piece of writing in which the writer describes his experience of crocodile hunting in Papua New Guinea. When you have read it, answer the questions that follow.

The Crocodile Hunter

I closed my eyes and shook my head, perhaps in the vain hope that this whole expedition would turn out to be a bad dream. But shaking my head was not a good idea, because it started the canoe rocking dangerously. I steadied the boat with my hands, and drew a deep breath. 'OK, Jack, if that did happen,
5 and we ended up in the water, what should I do?'

Jack paused. 'Well,' he said, 'whatever you do, don't splash about, because that'll get him excited.' He was still sweeping the waterline with his torch. 'What you should do is dive under and swim away. Crocs rarely bite underwater and he's unlikely to follow you.'

10 I wanted to be absolutely clear on these tips. 'So don't splash, and dive, dive, dive.'

'That's right.'

I had noted that he'd said crocs *rarely* bite underwater and that it was *unlikely* to follow me, but I didn't pursue these points because the entire
15 scenario was too horrible to imagine. I fell quiet, leaving Jack to continue scanning the water for swamp monsters while I digested this information.

This whole escapade had been preposterous from the start. If you chose to venture into a remote swamp in search of crocodiles, you might reasonably opt to do so with rather more equipment than a torch, a broom and a ball of
20 twine. A gun might be handy, for a start. You might also do so in a vessel of solid construction. I was thinking of something made of thick metal, preferably a boat that was also nippy, with a large engine enabling a fast get-away in case of difficulty. But here I was in a cumbersome wooden canoe forever in danger of capsizing, a boat that a large male crocodile might rationally mistake as a
25 competitor, a boat that could be flipped over and splintered with one whip of such a croc's giant tail.

I closed my eyes again, but didn't shake my head this time. The end was not difficult to imagine. Our aggressor would gobble us up with a few snaps of its jaws and use the boat's splinters as toothpicks. And the only thing we had to
30 defend ourselves with was a home-made wooden broom.

From *The Crocodile Hunter* by Steve and Terri Irwin

1 The writer describes the way he reacts to the situation. What do the following phrases show about his mood?
   - 'I closed my eyes and shook my head'
   - 'I steadied the boat with my hands, and drew a deep breath.'
   - 'I fell quiet.'

2 The tone of a piece of writing can often be described in different ways. Choose one of the following descriptions which *best* suits the tone of the passage:
   a It is very <u>serious</u> because Jack is showing just how dangerous the situation is.
   b The writing is full of <u>suspense</u> because Jack is warning how horrible it will be if an accident happens.
   c The writing is very <u>humorous</u> in tone because phrases like 'don't splash about' show that Jack doesn't take the idea of an accident very seriously.
   d The tone is mixed: although it is quite <u>light-hearted</u>, as you can see from Jack's responses, it is also quite <u>tense</u>, as you can tell the writer is worried.

3 Look at the final paragraph. The writer uses a phrase that makes the tone seem to be very serious: 'The end was not difficult to imagine.'
   a Explain how the writer's choice of words in the final two sentences makes the tone more light-hearted.
   b Rewrite the third sentence of the paragraph, changing the words to make the tone seem frightening.

Your own writing

You are now going to produce your own piece of writing. Remind yourself about the work you did when exploring *Into the Heart of Borneo* on pages 40–3 and *Service with a snarl* on pages 36–8. You explored how writers:
   - shape writing into paragraphs to help the reader follow their ideas easily
   - select interesting detail and vocabulary to describe places and people
   - use a variety of sentence types.

Follow these steps when you are planning your text:

Step 1

Think of a real place you have visited or live in, and imagine that your reader does not know the places you are describing.

Step 2

Choose an aspect of that place to write about. For example, in *Service with a snarl* the writer chose to comment on the way a group of people – waiters – behave. You might choose to focus on people in the place you choose. In *Into the Heart of Borneo* the writer chose to describe something that happened in Borneo that summed up what life is like in the jungle there.

Step 3

Before you start, think about the tone of your writing:
- do you wish to criticise or praise the place?
- do you want to write something that will make the reader smile in the same way that the description of life in the jungle of Borneo was intended to do?

When you have an idea for what to write, spend some time planning how you will shape the writing into paragraphs to help the reader follow your ideas easily. Remind yourself of the way *Service with a snarl* on page 36 was divided into short paragraphs and how the writer used a very short, single-sentence paragraph for effect.

Step 4

As you write you should focus on:
- selecting interesting detail and vocabulary to describe places and people
- highlighting important detail in short, simple sentences.

You are advised to:
- spend time considering different ideas before selecting one
- make a plan of how to structure your piece into beginning, middle and end
- write a first draft, keeping a careful eye on length.

Step 5

When you have written a first draft, you should let others read it and seek advice on:
- the way you paragraph it
- your use of short, simple sentences
- your use of figurative language.

In the light of what they say, make any changes that will make your writing more effective. Then produce a final version.

3 Influence and argument

The bigger picture

In this unit you will read a range of media and non-fiction texts. You will investigate how designers, writers and speakers use images and words to influence their readers. At the end of the unit you will show your understanding of a range of techniques through the analysis of two texts.

WHAT? You will:
- recognise how speech is used to influence readers
- examine how images and words are used to influence readers
- learn to use techniques of persuasion and argument in your own speech and writing

HOW? by:
- reflecting on the significance of words, body language and tone of voice in speech
- analysing a range of media texts
- examining and using a range of techniques used in speech and writing

WHY? because:
- increased awareness of the effects of words, body language and tone of voice helps you to become a more effective communicator
- it is important to recognise the power and influence of media images
- a better understanding of writing techniques will help you to become a more aware reader and a more effective writer.

The words you choose

The words we choose can have a huge effect on other people. We have the power to influence their thoughts and actions, but only if we choose our words carefully.

Activity 1

1 a What do you do when you want to get someone to do or think a certain thing? Do you:

Have a tantrum?   Bully?   Sulk?   Bribe?   Something else?

  b What might the last one be? What kind of cartoon could you draw to illustrate it?

2 Think about the situations described below. With a partner, decide which response is the most appropriate and why.

Situation 1

You walk into class five minutes after the lesson has started. To avoid getting into trouble, do you:

a walk to your desk, sit down noisily and ask a friend what you should be doing?

b wait until the teacher stops talking. Apologise and explain why you are late?

Situation 2

You want to leave your last lesson five minutes early as you are playing in a match and need to start on time. To get what you want, do you:

a tell your teacher you have to go five minutes early?

b ask if you can leave early and explain why?

Situation 3

You want to watch TV but your dad wants you to do your homework NOW.

To persuade your dad to let you watch TV now, do you:

a explain what you have to do and how long it will take you?

b pretend you've already done it and wave an empty schoolbag in front of him?

Activity 2

Help Beth and Adrian to get what they want. Write a script for each of the following situations, showing how they could successfully deal with a tricky situation.

Situation 4

Beth wants to go to a friend's sleepover on Wednesday night. Her mum hasn't yet decided whether to let her go. She wants Beth to tidy her bedroom because her aunt is coming to stay at the weekend and will be sleeping in that room. How could Beth influence her mother's decision?

Situation 5

Adrian has done well in his exams. His dad has bought him a computer game he doesn't want. He really wants the most recent version of the same game. This would cost another £10. How could Adrian persuade his dad to exchange it for the new game?

Body language

As well as using words that are most likely to influence others, it is important to get your message across with your **facial expressions** and **body movements**. This is called body language.

Activity 3

1 Talk with a partner about how you could use your facial expressions and body movements to show the following:
   - I agree
   - I'm not sure about that
   - I'm happy
   - I don't want to be noticed
   - I disagree
   - I'm not listening to you
   - I'm very sad
   - I want to be noticed.

2 Now think of the actions you might use to accompany the following words:

> Remember, children, to look right and left and right again before crossing the road.

> The car missed her by this much.

> Then he slammed the book down on the desk.

> They gave it the thumbs up.

Activity 4

This activity will help to increase your awareness of details of another person's body language.

1 a Sit or stand facing your partner. Name yourselves A and B. A takes the lead and makes a series of different body movements but does not change their facial expression. B has to mirror the movements exactly. Do this for two minutes before changing roles.

b Now do the same with facial expressions. Remember, one of you takes the lead and the other has to mirror the expressions exactly.

Highlight thinking

Emotional Intelligence

Activities 1–4 will help you to develop your awareness of what others may be thinking or feeling. This is called **Emotional Intelligence** or 'EI'. EI also means recognising how you feel and communicating it successfully to others. An awareness of expression and body language will help you to:

- understand others better
- communicate your own feelings and ideas more effectively.

2 Now you will draw on what you know about body language.

a Join another pair. Start by talking about how you would identify each of the following 'types' in the playground by their body language:

- the bully
- the victim
- the smoker
- the boaster
- the flirt
- the teacher on duty
- a year 7 student on their first day
- a year 11 student on their last day.

b Each person in the group should pose as one of these 'types', using the appropriate body language. This is called a 'still'. The others should guess which 'type' it is. If they guess correctly, move on. If not, give advice on how the pose could be improved.

3 Your group is going to create a role-play that involves only body language. This is called a 'mime'. You should not speak.

a Choose a situation that might occur at breaktime. Decide which characters are involved.

b Talk about different ways in which the situation might develop.

c Then start the mime, making it up as you go along within the general structure you have discussed. This type of role-play is called 'improvisation'. Your improvisation should last 2–3 minutes.

Feedback

Read all of the instructions in this feedback before you begin. Take it in turns to improvise your scenes in front of the whole class. Do not give any introduction to your role-play – your body language should tell the story. After each role-play, the class should discuss:

- what they think was happening
- the personalities of the different characters in the role-play
- the different relationships between the characters.

The discussion should be based on what the class learnt about the situation from the characters' body language.

Listen carefully when your group's role-play is being discussed. You may need to answer questions or give extra information. At the end of the discussion, make notes on:

- the positive things people said about your role-play
- how your group could make more effective use of body language.

Tone of voice

So far, you have thought about the words you choose and the way you use body language to convey meaning. You are now going to consider how you say the words you have chosen: the **tone of voice** that you choose. Your tone of voice is decided by:

- pace – the speed at which you speak
- pitch – the frequency you use, e.g. high pitch, even pitch, low pitch
- volume – the amount of sound you make.

How you say something can be more important than what you say. Pace, pitch and volume can make what you say more or less effective. They need to fit with the words you are speaking.

Before doing Activity 5, talk with a partner about people who you think use tone of voice effectively. Decide what it is about the way they speak that makes them effective.

Activity 5

1 What pace and pitch might you use to show:
- excitement? • anger? • sadness?

2 List two examples of times when you might want to:
- speak loudly • speak quietly.

3 With a partner, practise saying statements A–D below, using different paces, pitches and volumes. For each one, decide which way is the:
- funniest • most appropriate.

A 'The budgie is dead.'
B 'Shoot, man! Get the ball in the net!'
C 'This is the BBC News at midday on Tuesday, the thirteenth of June.'
D 'Come in quietly and get your pens and books out.'

Copy and complete the chart below to show your decisions. An example is done for you, though you may not agree with it.

Statement	Style	Pace	Pitch	Volume
A	Funniest	slow	low	loud
	Most appropriate			
B	Funniest			
	Most appropriate			

Using visual images to influence

You have considered how the words you speak and the way you say them can influence others. Advertisers and campaign managers are also very aware that **images** can make a big difference. Many advertising campaigns which try to influence people's opinions, focus on choosing effective images. Sometimes they are designed to shock.

Activity 6

Examine closely the poster on page 63.

1 Choose three of these adjectives that you would use to describe this poster:
- horrible • shocking • disgusting • funny
- sick • frightening • amusing • pathetic.

Explain why you have chosen each of these three adjectives. You could use the following sentence structure to help you explain:

I have chosen the adjective _____ to describe this poster because _____ .

2 List three things that the designers of this poster have done to give the poster a strong visual impact.

3 What do you think the designers of this poster are trying to achieve? Give at least two reasons for your answer.

When using a strong visual image to influence people, advertisers often use **association**. This is where they rely on the reader to make a number of mental connections between ideas and feelings. Examine the next poster closely. The notes beside it will help you understand how association works.

Words used to promote smoking → 'pack of lies' → suggests the words used on the cigarettes are lies

Letters 'R.I.P' used → usually found on a gravestone → death → suggests cigarettes cause death

Colour yellow is used → also the colour of nicotine → makes you think of nicotine-stained fingers

Words 'pack of lies' → box looks like a pack of cards → you use cards for a card trick → suggests smokers are being tricked

Colour black is used → associated with death → suggests cigarettes cause death

 Activity 7

You are going to create your own anti-smoking poster. Your aim is to:

Shock your reader *or* Make your point using association of ideas.

If you are very ambitious, you could do both!

Follow the stages below.

1 Brainstorm a range of ideas to do with getting your anti-smoking message across in a visual image.

2 Decide which words, if any, you want to use on your poster.

3 Lightly sketch the outline of your poster in pencil. Think about:
- how to give your image maximum impact
- where to place the word(s).

4 Decide which colours to use. Remember we associate different things with different colours.

5 Ask a partner if they can think of ways you could improve your poster. If you like their idea(s), use them.

6 Complete your poster using colours for maximum impact.

 Sharpen punctuation

Abbreviations

Full stops are sometimes used to mark an abbreviated word or words, for example:
- R.I.P. = rest in peace
- e.g. = *exempli gratia* (Latin words meaning 'for example')
- U.K. = United Kingdom

In recent years there has been a move away from the use of the full stop in abbreviations, e.g.
- CD   compact disc
- DVD   digital versatile disc
- BBC   British Broadcasting Corporation.

You will come across both forms in written texts.

Work out what the following abbreviations stand for. Use a dictionary to help you if you are not sure.
- CIA
- EEC
- a.m.
- p.m.
- FIFA
- GCSE
- JFK
- M.P.
- P.T.O.
- ROM
- RSPCA
- s.a.e.
- SPF
- VCR
- W.C.

 Progress check

So far in this unit you have learnt about:
- how words, body language and tone of voice can influence others
- how visual images can prompt association of ideas and feelings
- how visual images can be combined with words to influence.

Study the poster on page 66 and answer the following questions:

1 What is the poster advertising?

2 Describe the image used. What does the image suggest about the place?

3 What do the words in quotation marks suggest about the place?

4 List the features of the poster which might make you think of a newly released film?

5 Think about your answers to questions 1 to 4. Explain two or three ways the poster tries to make people want to visit Warwick Castle.

6 Check your answers with the answers given on page 81.

7 Create and present a 20-second radio advertisement to persuade people to visit Warwick Castle. You will need to:
- decide what you want to say
- decide how you should say it
- practise your presentation several times before trying it out on a partner
- take into account their feedback before presenting to a group of students.

New for 2004

WARWICK GHOSTS
ALIVE

✠ WARWICK CASTLE ✠

Britain's Greatest Mediaeval Experience

"SUSPENSE HAS NEVER BEEN MORE ENTERTAINING"
"THE MEDIAEVAL CASTLE PROVIDES A BREATHTAKING LOCATION" "A SLICK, SHARP THRILLER"
"THE SPECIAL EFFECTS ARE TRULY HAUNTING" "UNMISSABLE"

OPENS 1st APRIL

This new live action experience is an additional charge to the normal entry fee. To guarantee admission book in advance at WWW.WARWICK-CASTLE.CO.UK or call 0870 442 2375.

This experience is designed to be spooky with an element of surprise. As a result, it may not be suitable for children under 8 years old or visitors with heart conditions or high blood pressure.

NOT SHOWING AT YOUR LOCAL CINEMA

The Tussauds Group

Using words to influence the reader

You have thought about how what we say can influence the way people respond to us and how advertisers use images and words to influence people. Now you are going to think about how writers use words to influence readers in reviews. Reviews can be written about books, films, plays, computer games, concerts and many other things. Reviews can be positive (good) or negative (bad), or a mixture of both. A review usually:

- gives you information on what the subject is about
- gives you the writer's opinion on the subject.

Activity 8

Read the following review of Philip Pullman's *His Dark Materials* books. Some of the main features are highlighted for you.

List five things the writer says which give a positive (good) impression of this book.

A darker read ...

short, snappy command

written in the present tense

compares it to other well-known books

tells you something about the main characters

tells you something about the story

If you haven't read *His Dark Materials* by Philip Pullman already, do it now. Even Hollywood has picked up on it and there's a film in the pipeline.

It's a trilogy, like *Lord of the Rings*, with 1,300 pages all told.

On the way you meet a cast of characters to rival *Harry Potter*, including a three-fingered philosopher, prowling, life-sucking Specters, and a shaman with a hole in his head.

Just like in *Lord of the Rings*, it is the little people who save the day. Our heroes are two of the bravest children you will ever meet – the independent, mischievous and ever-capable Lyra Belacqua and her friend William Parry, who is quiet, brooding and strong.

Together they journey out of their own worlds aided by many unlikely friends – including an armoured polar bear – and are preyed on by some of the most terrifying enemies anyone could imagine.

The adventure is gripping, sometimes laugh-out-loud funny, but you will cry! At times you'll have to tear yourself away from the page, unable to take it any longer, and then quickly return for more.

And finally, when all three books are finished, you will find yourself smiling and thinking about things you have never thought about before, things like dark matter, parallel universes and what happens when we die. It is a thrilling, charming, moving, scary, magical story. It is blummin' brilliant!

predicts how the reader will react to it

uses a range of adjectives

uses non-standard English to sum up own opinion

Activity 9

1 Read the following review of the film *Peter Pan*.

★ FILM REVIEWS ★

Peter Pan (PG)

THE TIMELESS STORY AS YOU'VE NEVER SEEN IT BEFORE.

PETER PAN

The first live-action version of *Peter Pan* is a near-perfect example of how to mess up a sure thing. This movie has everything going for it.

Firstly, it's a well-loved children's story that has hardly been touched by film producers before now. Secondly, it rides on the wave of popularity currently enjoyed by kid-lit in general, thanks to the wizard Potter. Thirdly, it's got pirates in it and – take a bow, Johnny Depp – pirates are the new cool.

Unfortunately, while *Pirates of the Caribbean* and the Harry Potter franchise have succeeded by either subverting or remaining religiously true to their inspirations, *Peter Pan* flunks it by not having enough faith in its source material.

Visually, the movie is almost flawless, capturing the magical atmosphere of Neverland and the open nursery window perfectly. However, an injection of unwanted slapstick, a charmless script and – worst of all – an American Peter Pan, turn what could have been a definitive adaptation into just another Hollywood-ised blockbuster. Although director Hogan touches on some of the book's themes of adolescence and loneliness, nothing is allowed to get in the way of the expensive, but frequently ropey CGI (computer generated images) effects.

Final verdict

Picture	★★★★	Extras	★★
Sound	★★★★★	Value	★★★
Entertainment	★★		

Overall ★★

Disappointing adaptation with randomly constructed extras.

2 Find and write down examples of the following features:

- compares this to other well-known films
- uses the present tense
- refers to some of the characters
- makes the hero sound unattractive
- uses adjectives to make it seem bad
- uses non-standard English
- sums it up.

3 What impression of the film does this review create? How might it influence a reader?

4 Do you think the 'Final Verdict' section is a good way to end a review? What makes it good or bad? Give reasons for your answer.

Activity 10

You are going to write a review of a book, a film, a computer game, a website or a TV programme.

Sharpen spelling

Spelling complex words

When spelling more complex words, it is often helpful if you can identify the root word. A root word is a word to which prefixes and suffixes may be added to make other words. Here are three examples taken from the passage:

unable	independent	prowling
↓ ↓	↓ ↓ ↓	↓ ↓
prefix root	prefix root suffix	root suffix

Copy the following words and identify the prefixes, roots and suffixes, as shown in the examples above.

- chewing • remaining • fingered • powerful
- unlikely • quickly • finally • thrilling
- magical • finished

This technique will help you to see the parts that make up the whole word, and this, in turn, will help you to memorise the spelling.

Your review can be either positive, like the review of *His Dark Materials*, or negative, like the review of *Peter Pan*. To write your review, follow the steps described on page 70.

Step 1

Choose the subject of your review. Collect ideas for your review, using the prompts below:

How you think the reader will react to it

Brief outline of plot or contents

Your opinion of it

Non-standard English phrases that make it sound good or bad

Name of text

Brief information about characters

How you would sum it up

Adjectives to describe it

What you think of the hero or heroine

Other things it could be compared with

Step 2

Decide on the order in which you are going to organise your ideas. For example:

- start with a short, snappy introduction
- then write a short outline of the plot or contents (no more than three sentences)
- next, write about the main character(s)
- after that, give your opinion and say how you think your reader would react
- finally, sum up your thoughts in words or use a 'Final Verdict' chart.

Remember to write in the present tense.

Feedback

Once you have written the first draft of your review, ask a partner to read it. Your partner should tell you which of the following things you did or did not do. They could copy this list and then put a tick or cross beside each point.

a Give a clear idea of what it is about.
b Tell me something about the main characters.
c Compare it to other things.
d Use adjectives to describe it.
e Tell me your opinion.
f Say how you think your reader will react.
g Sum up your thoughts.
h Write in the present tense.

Use the feedback from your partner, and any further ideas you have had, to help you to add to and improve your review. When you are sure it is as good as it can be, redraft it and either draw or suggest a picture that could accompany it.

How writers persuade readers

In the reviews you have just studied, the writers were trying to influence the opinions of their readers. Sometimes writers are trying to achieve something more specific: they are trying to persuade their readers to do something. In the following article on pages 72–3 the writer is trying to persuade readers to buy tickets for a dog show. To achieve this, the writer uses a range of persuasive techniques.

Activity 11

Read the following article closely. Answer the questions below to help you identify the techniques the writer uses.

1 Write down two sentences in which the writer speaks directly to the reader by using the second person – *you*.

2 Choose and write down two phrases that the writer uses to make the show sound:
   - exciting
   - enjoyable.

3 Give two examples where the writer creates humour through:
   - words
   - pictures.

4 Give two examples where the writer uses a rhetorical question to involve the reader.

5 The writer ends the first four paragraphs with an exclamation mark. Why do you think she does this?

6 How does the writer use association of ideas when she writes about 'the massively popular Pup Idol'?

7 Give an example where the writer uses a list to make the show sound lively.

8 What are the connections between the pictures on page 73 and the written text?

9 Why do you think the list of charities has been included in this article?

10 Do you think the writer of this article would be successful in her attempt to persuade dog lovers to go to the show? Give at least two reasons for your answer.

The most fun your dog can have ... almost!

Take part in the Wag & Bone Show and give your dog the best day out he or she has ever had. Best of all, you'll be helping less fortunate dogs just by turning up!

The Wag & Bone Show is getting closer and while you could just turn up on the day and have a really great time, you and your dog could become one of the main attractions instead!

There are several elements you can only enter in advance and – unlike many other events – there's nothing stuffy about Wag & Bone!

You can use creativity to make up for any lack of expertise!

The massively popular Pup Idol proved completely inspirational and could easily develop into a completely new genre of canine competition. There are almost no rules. You just have two minutes to entertain the judges and the crowd – and the competition attracted an incredible diversity of entries that ensured the ringside was always packed and the audience frequently moved to tears of laughter!

My personal highlights were the singing dog, the tap-dancing dog and of course the magnificent Suggs the Staffie doing almost a *Crimewatch* reconstruction of rescuing a cat!

Perhaps your dog has a party piece you can script into a two-minute audition? You can bring props, in fact the more complicated the act, the more impressive!

However – sometimes the simple things will capture the crowd's attention.

Singing, talking, dancing, counting, acting – let your imagination run wild. Get your entry in and start working on your act.

Because we had so many brilliant dancing dogs last year – this year they are getting their own competition and ring. If you want

to take part, send off a.s.a.p. for an entry form. If you're interested in getting into this emerging sport, there will be master classes so you can have a go at doggie dancing.

The lady who had her hair dyed to match her tri-colour Cavalier was inspirational – and it was a good look – I'm sure other people will copy it! And the Irish Water Spaniel woman with the hairy boots and tail attachment – she absolutely summed up the spirit of the occasion in visual form.

I hope your appetite is whetted and you're up for joining in – don't worry if you're shy. Just by coming and watching other braver souls you are adding to the success of this unique event.

And don't forget – you need to reserve your tickets early this year. When the show starts to be advertised in the *Daily Mail* there's every chance it will sell out.

Do you look like your dog? Or does your dog look like anyone famous?

Our look-alike competition last year was absolutely brilliant. The naturals are very

far and few – but I have to say how much I admire all those wonderful people who went to tremendous lengths to look like their dogs.

Proceeds from the Wag & Bone Show will benefit all these animal welfare charities

From Dogs Today, July 2004

How speakers persuade listeners

People who speak in public are often trying to persuade their listeners. In the following speech, the speaker is trying to encourage his listeners to become organ donors. He presents a clear argument for the listener to follow.

Activity 12

1 Read the transcript of the speech *Become an Organ Donor* closely. The following annotations describe the techniques the speaker is using. Match these annotations to the numbers on the speech.

   A Ideas are grouped into threes for extra impact.

   B The audience is directly addressed as 'you'.

   C Rhetorical questions are asked to involve the audience.

   D A picture of real people is created to make the subject more real.

   E Ideas are repeated to give extra impact.

   F Direct, dramatic opening statement to grab the audience's attention.

   G Words are chosen to appeal to the audience's feelings.

   H The speaker shows he understands the audience's feelings.

2 There are three main sections to this speech:

   a the **Introduction**, in which the speaker grabs the audience's attention and outlines the problem.

   b the **Body**, in which the speaker shows how the problem could be solved.

   c the **Conclusion**, in which the speaker sums up the points made.

Identify by line number where you think each of these three sections starts and ends.

3 In his argument the speaker combines a mixture of:

- **Facts:** things that can be proved to be true
- **Opinions:** points of view that cannot be proved to be true or false.

Read lines 10–15 and list three facts and three opinions that the writer uses in these lines.

4 Would the words in this speech persuade you to become an organ donor? With a partner, work out how the speaker could best use tone of voice (pace, pitch and volume) and body language to help persuade the audience. Experiment with saying parts of the speech in different ways to help you decide.

Become an Organ Donor

1 — By this time tomorrow, 12 people in America who are alive right now will be
dead. Not because they were in a car wreck,
not because they were gunned down,
not because their time had come,

5 not even because they weren't in the hospital,
but simply because they couldn't be given a life-saving transplant in time.

2 12 people will die because the organ transplant they need will not be possible.
Yet there are more than enough potential donors.
The problem is, those potential donors die without leaving instructions.

10 And this is a problem on an enormous scale.
Currently, nearly 60,000 Americans are waiting for a life-saving organ transplant.
Every day 12 people will die while awaiting a transplant.

3 And every 16 minutes another name is added to the waiting list.
But here is the real tragedy:

15 it really is so easy to fix this problem.
There is an amazing network across the United States that links hospitals with
one another and can match donors with patients.
The one thing that's missing is a pool of donors.
So how can you help?

4 20 Well, first, you need to make the decision that when the time comes, you would
like to help someone else.

5 — And that's quite something to go through.
But remember, one day you may be relying on someone to do the same for you.
Once you've made the decision, you need to make sure your family knows.

25 You will also want to use donor cards.

6 — How do you go about getting a Donor Card?
Visit the National Kidney Foundation's web page on donation.
And that really is all there is to it.
The fact is, there's nothing but good that can come from this.

30 Right now, in Arizona, there is a little girl waiting for a kidney.

7 — Right now, in Maine, there's a father of three young kids who is waiting for a
liver transplant.
If they can have an organ, their story will be a happy one,
and the sooner more people sign up,

35 including you,
the sooner those waiting lists will go down,

8 — and the sooner those people will get the life they were meant to live.

* You can be an organ donor at any age in the UK, but if you're under 16, your parent or guardian must also agree.

Activity 13

1 Choose one of the following situations.

- Your year group has decided to choose a charity to support. Prepare and present a speech persuading them to support the charity of your choice.
- Your year group is going to vote on where to go for an end-of-year trip. Prepare and present the script for a speech persuading them to vote for the place of your choice.

Your speech should be 2–3 minutes long. Follow these tips to help you:

Spectacular speeches

☆ Choose 3–4 key points to develop.

☆ Grab your audience's attention straight away with a strange fact, a question or a challenge.

☆ Aim to have 3–5 cards on which you note your key points and how you will develop them.

☆ Use the speech-making techniques you identified in Activity 12, such as groups of three, rhetorical questions and repetition for effect.

☆ Use body language and tone of voice to add impact to what you say.

☆ End strongly: sum up your ideas, return to your opening point for emphasis or leave your audience with a new point to think about.

 **Sharpen punctuation**

Using Commas to pause

Commas can be used in speeches to show when to pause.

Re-read lines 1–6 of *Become an Organ Donor* on page 75. With a partner, talk about:

- what the commas tell you about the ways these lines should be spoken
- why you think a new line is started after each comma in the second sentence.

Rewrite the following speech made by a Year Head. Place the commas where you think the speaker should pause and start new lines when appropriate.

> By this time tomorrow several students in your year will have failed to hand in homework. Not because they couldn't do the work not because they were visiting their sick grandmothers not because their younger brother had placed their school bag in the bath not even because their pet hamster had died unexpectedly but simply because they couldn't be bothered to.

2 Once you have prepared your speech, practise in front of a friend or speak into a tape recorder or in front of a mirror. You will need to practise your speech three or four times before you are ready to present it to a larger group.

 Feedback

1 In a group of three or four, decide what are the *three* most important things about a good speech. Place them in order of importance.

2 Assess each speech you hear using these three criteria. For each one, award a mark of 1–3, where 3 is the best mark. Decide on a comment to give the speaker. Your comment should focus on what they have done well and on how they could improve.

Progress check

So far in this unit you have learnt about:

- how words, body language and tone of voice can influence others
- how visual images can prompt associations of ideas and feelings
- how visual images can be combined with words to influence the reader
- how writers use words to create positive and negative reviews
- how writers and speakers use words to persuade.

Look back through the unit and the work you have done. Write a report on your work so far. Use this frame to help you organise your comments.

(write your name) is a(n) _(choose an adjective to describe yourself)_ pupil. He/She has _(describe how hard you have worked)_ whilst studying the unit 'Influence and argument'. He/She seemed to be most interested whilst learning about _(name the part you were most interested in)_ . His/Her best piece of written work was _(name your best piece of written work)_ . He/She did least well when learning about _(name the part you did least well in)_ . This was because _(explain why you did least well in this)_ .

Award yourself a medal according to how well you think you have done.

 Bronze: I would like to review some of the things we have studied to help me understand them.

 Silver: I am unsure about some elements of what we have learnt.

 Gold: I understand everything we have studied and am confident putting it into practice.

Making a point forcefully

When making a case for or against something, the writer presents the reader with an argument. Many of the techniques used in the speech on organ donation are also used by writers when they argue a particular point of view.

Activity 14

Read the magazine article on page 78.

Find and write down examples of the following techniques:

a addresses the reader directly as 'you'
b an opinion
c a group of three
d an example to support an opinion
e an exclamation for effect
f a rhetorical question.

Pop Idol or Flop Idol?

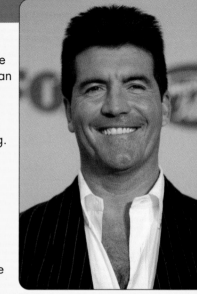

Have you ever watched *Pop Idol*? Talk about bad TV. Every week, twice a week, it fills the screen and churns my stomach.

It's full of pathetic wannabes queuing up for hours, shrieking with exaggerated excitement and endlessly applying make-up to cover their spotty adolescent faces. There's the group of girls from Coventry who can't dance in time and sing out of tune or the five lads from Newcastle who plan on being the next best-boy-band-in-the-world. How original! They try, poor dears, smiling vacantly and pleading pathetically, to please the row of sour-faced oldies, but all the judges can do is sneer and belittle their efforts.

The worse judge of all is Simon Cowell. What a smug, self-satisfied pig of a man he is. I'd like to see him try to sing in front of an audience. All he can do is sit there and criticise. 'You are the worst singer I've ever heard,' he says for the tenth time, yawning rudely. Well, he's not the only one yawning. Perhaps it's him who needs a course in originality!

And, just when you think the yawning's over and the great British public has voted for the next mega-failure of the pop world, what happens? *The X Factor*, that's what. The same thing but this time with grannies and grandads as well! Time, I think, to give up, chill out and reach for the DVD.

Using bias

One main feature of the magazine article that is not found in the speech on organ donation is **bias**. Bias is shown in the article when the writer allows her personal feelings to influence her judgement.

- She could have said:
  chattering with nervous excitement
- She said:
  shrieking with exaggerated excitement

What does the second phrase tell you about the way the writer views the contestants?

The writer's bias is clear in:
- the words writers use to put across a particular point of view
- the selection of detail the writer chooses to make.

Re-read the following extract and talk about the questions that surround it, to help you become more aware of the bias.

Sharpen spelling

Words within words

One way of remembering spellings is to find words within words. Here are some examples of words taken from the article:

- ex**item**ent
- ap**ply**ing
- adole**scent**
- ori**gin**al
- va**can**tly
- p**lead**ing
- au**die**nce

Copy the words below and circle the words within them to help you remember them. You can circle more than one word within a word.

- agriculture
- business
- compromise
- desperate
- environment
- foreign
- glisten
- honourable
- instrument
- judgement
- knowledge
- lasagne
- merchandise
- opportunity
- neighbourhood

1 How could the writer have reworded this phrase to create a better impression of the contestants?

2 Is this a fair or unfair description?

3 Why do you think the writer does not mention any good performers?

4 What tone is being used here?

> It's full of pathetic wannabes queuing up for hours, shrieking with exaggerated excitement and endlessly applying make-up to cover their spotty adolescent faces. There's the group of girls from Coventry who can't dance in time and sing out of tune or the five lads from Newcastle who plan on being the next best-boy-
> 5 band-in-the-world. How original! They try, poor dears, smiling vacantly and pleading pathetically, to please the row of sour-faced oldies, but all the judges can do is sneer and belittle their efforts.

5 Do you think the judges always react in this way?

Using bias can be an effective technique in presenting an argument but, as a reader, you need to make sure you can see through it.

Activity 15

You are going to write an article for 'Question of the week'. Follow the steps below.

1 Choose a subject you feel strongly about. It could be to do with:
- teachers
- sport
- television
- school hours
- religion
- celebrities.

This is your opportunity to get your feelings off your chest and persuade others that your point of view is the right one. You could have positive or negative feelings towards your chosen subject.

2 Aim to write 150–250 words. Plan your ideas in four paragraphs.

Paragraph 1: state your point of view clearly and strongly.
Paragraph 2: choose one main point to develop in detail.
Paragraph 3: choose a different main point to develop in detail.
Paragraph 4: sum up your ideas, repeat your opening point or introduce a completely new point.

3 When you write your first draft, experiment with a range of techniques such as rhetorical questions, repetition for effect, groups of three and exclamations. Address your reader as 'you' and give examples to support your opinions.

4 Ask a partner to read your first draft and to check that you have:
- organised your writing into four paragraphs
- used some of the techniques listed in point 3 above
- made your point clearly and with impact.

5 Think about what your partner has said and make improvements to your draft before you write out your final copy.

Assessment task

> ### Hamburgers: friend or foe?
> You are going to examine a media text about hamburgers using the skills you have learnt in this unit. You will be assessed on the way you:
> - identify and select facts
> - use spelling techniques you have learnt
> - examine different aspects of a media text
> - evaluate the effectiveness of a media text.
>
> Read the text on page 81 closely and then answer the questions below.

Facts

1 a Copy and complete this sentence:

A fact is something that ...

b Find and list five facts that the writer uses to develop his argument.

Introduction, body and conclusion

2 a Re-read the opening sentence. What effect do you think the writer is hoping to have on the reader?

b Re-read lines 24-37. List the main points the writer makes here.

c Re-read the last paragraph. Why do you think the writer has finished the article in this way?

Techniques

3 Find and copy two examples of the writer:

a using rhetorical questions

c using a group of three.

b addressing the reader directly

Spelling

4 a Copy the words below. Find and highlight the word within each one.

- protein
- average
- produce
- important
- vegetation
- environmental
- properly
- cleared
- practices

b Build at least six words from the root word *consider*.

Visual image

5 a Look closely at the photograph in the article. Choose two adjectives from the following list which you would use to describe this image.

- horrible
- shocking
- disgusting
- funny
- sick
- frightening
- amusing
- pathetic

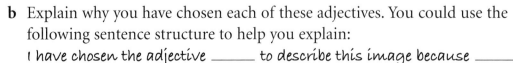

b Explain why you have chosen each of these adjectives. You could use the following sentence structure to help you explain:

I have chosen the adjective _____ to describe this image because _____.

c Do you think this was a good choice of image for this article? Give at least two reasons to explain your opinion.

A Large Order of Fries and 500 Gallons of Water – To Go

Believe it or not, it can take more than 500 gallons (1900 litres) of water and five pounds (2.3 kg) of grain to make four quarter-pound hamburgers. And in some areas, the amount of water could be 2500 gallons (9500 litres)!
5 Seem like a lot? The fact is, producing beef is not the most efficient way to convert natural resources into protein for our diets. That's because it takes a lot of land, food and water to raise a herd of cattle. And when you compare the resources it takes to produce beef versus
10 other foods, you can see one reason why a 'beefy' society like the United States uses so many of the Earth's resources. While chomping away on your next burger, consider the following:

- The average American consumes the equivalent of
15   about 120 quarter-pounders every year.

- Over 70 per cent of the grain produced in the United States is fed to livestock.

- Some experts estimate that it takes 40 per cent more fossil fuels to make a pound of protein from beef
20   than from soybeans.

- In some areas it can take as much as 10–100 times more water to produce a pound of beef than a pound of wheat.

Besides using enormous amounts of water, grain and
25 energy, raising beef can mean a loss of natural vegetation, packed-down soil and lots of cow manure that can contaminate rivers and streams. And in some parts of the world, forests are being cleared to make way for more cattle ranches or to grow crops to feed cattle.

30   So should you stop your burger binges? Before you decide, it's important to think about all sides of the issue and do your homework. For example, many people are working to improve grazing practices and make beef production more eco-friendly. Some nutritionists say
35 that lean beef can be a good source of protein in your diet. And lots of people earn their living by raising and selling beef.

Veggieburger or hamburger or both? It's a meaty dilemma, but only you can decide.

From *Windows on the Wild*

Evaluation

6 a What do you think the writer of this article is trying to achieve?
  b How successful do you think this article is? Give reasons for your answers.

Answers to the Progress check questions on page 65

1 The new 'experience' at Warwick Castle.
2 Castle walls at night with a ghostly face imprinted on them. The image suggests the place is frightening, ghostly and mysterious.
3 The words suggest the place is exciting and frightening.
4 Features: New for 2004, *Alive* printed as though it were the name of a film, quotations as though taken from reviews, the 8+ sign, the red strip with the words *Not showing* makes you think of *Now showing*.
5 You should explain why the images and words mentioned in questions 1–4 would make you want to visit.

81

4 Creating structures

The bigger picture

In this unit you will learn how texts are written and presented by exploring different types of texts, including a newspaper article, a formal letter and an information leaflet. You will then compare two texts on the same topic. You will also develop your research and note-making skills. At the end of the unit you will research and write a short biography of a famous person.

WHAT? **You will:**
- develop different ways of linking paragraphs
- explore different ways of grouping sentences into paragraphs
- learn how to address readers directly when writing texts
- learn how to make notes and use research skills to gather information

HOW? **by:**
- studying the organisation of a range of texts
- experimenting with ways of organising ideas in your own writing
- looking closely at texts where writers address their readers
- making notes in a variety of ways

WHY? **because:**
- studying the organisation of texts will improve your own skills as a writer
- learning how to address your readers will increase your range of writing styles
- making notes and using research skills will help you in all your school subjects.

The organisation and presentation of newspaper articles

Different kinds of texts are organised and presented in different ways. How they are organised depends on *why* they are written and *who* they are written for. For example, a recipe is organised in a logical way, with a list of ingredients followed by the various stages of preparation in an easy-to-follow sequence.

This article about a little girl attacked by an urban fox shows you how newspaper articles are organised and presented.

Read the article.

Fox attacks girl in her bedroom

Agony after it bites with razor teeth

by **Geoff Maynard**

1 **A girl of four was left in agony after being attacked by a fox as she slept in her bed.**

2 The animal plunged its razor-sharp teeth into Jessica Brown's arm after creeping through an open door at her home.

3 Her panic-stricken parents Richard Brown and his wife, Corinne Magnier, both 36, had been watching TV when they heard her screams.

4 They rushed up to the bedroom and chased the fox out of their home in Tufnell Park, north London. They believe the animal was attracted by the smell of chicken the family had eaten earlier.

5 English teacher Mr Brown explained: 'We heard a loud cry from Jessica's room and my wife dashed up and screamed at me to come.

6 'I ran upstairs and saw the beast. It ran to the top floor of the house. I chased it back down to the bathroom and it was on the window ledge but realised it couldn't jump from that height.'

7 Mr Brown chased the fox out of his house before returning to his daughter who was hysterical. 'Jessica's arm had big U-shaped teeth marks on it. The skin was broken and there was blood. We dashed to hospital where they put antiseptics on and gave her antibiotics,' he said.

8 Mr Brown branded Islington Council's response to the attack 'appalling'. He said the fox's lair was in the garden of a council-managed house next door, and had not been cleared for five years. He said: 'Every time I have phoned departments at the council they said it was not their job, or "nothing to do with us".

9 'We have got a dangerous animal living next door to my house. I think it is unacceptable.'

10 Islington Council said it planned to clear the garden and would seek specialist advice on dealing with urban foxes.

VICIOUS: An urban fox pounced on Jessica, above, who shows off her bite

From *The Daily Express*

Presentational devices

Newspaper articles use a variety of fonts and images to get their message across. Photographs, in particular, are an important feature in newspapers, and can often be as important as the words.

Activity 1

1 Estimate what proportion of the article is taken up by:
- the headline, sub-headline and strapline (the strapline gives the name of the writer)
- the two photographs
- the story.

2 Why do you think so much space is devoted to the headline and the photographs?

3 Look carefully at the photograph of the little girl. It has been taken from above. Why do you think the photographer did this and why did he ask her to pose in that way? What effect was this intended to have on the reader?

4 The other photograph is unlikely to be the fox involved in the story. Why do you think the newspaper chose this one?

5 The photograph of the fox is accompanied by a caption. What is the purpose of the caption?

6 Imagine that you want to use the photograph of the fox to capture some sympathy from readers. What caption could you write for the photograph that would change the way you react to the fox?

Language

To attract and interest readers, the writers of newspaper articles use language to make their stories vivid and effective. In the activity below you will examine ways in which language can be used.

Activity 2

1 a In what tense is most of the article written?
  b In what tense are the headline and sub-headline written?
  c What would the headline and sub-headline say if they were written in the same tense as the story?
  d Explain why the writer decided to write the headline and sub-headline in a different tense from the story.

2 Newspaper articles often contain quotations. This story quotes Mr Brown, the little girl's father. Sometimes it uses his exact words – direct speech – and sometimes it reports the gist of what he said – indirect or reported speech. Look at paragraph 8 from the story and identify the direct and indirect speech. How can you tell the difference?

> Mr Brown branded Islington Council's response to the attack 'appalling'.
> He said the fox's lair was in the garden of a council-managed house next door, and had not been cleared for five years. He said: 'Every time I have phoned departments at the council they said it was not their job, or "nothing to do with us".'

Why do you think the writer uses a mixture of direct and indirect speech, rather than just choosing one?

In this example, the writer uses single inverted commas for direct speech, and then double inverted commas for someone else's words within the direct speech. But you could also do it the other way around – double inverted commas followed by single.

Sharpen punctuation

Using single and double inverted commas
Quotations and direct speech should be written within inverted commas. Inverted commas can be either single (' ...') or double ("...").

When a speaker quotes something said by another person, you then need to use both types of inverted commas, for example: 'I was so happy when they told me "We're getting married".'

> 'Every time I have phoned departments at the council they said it was not their job, or "nothing to do with us".'

Mr Brown's words are in single inverted commas.

The council's words are quoted within Mr Brown's words and double quote marks are used to show this.

Now punctuate these sentences, using double and single inverted commas as appropriate.
   a The girl said: When the Queen said I am very proud of you I felt ten feet tall.
   b In response to the judge's question the police officer said, I heard the defendant shout You're dead! at the victim, moments before the attack.

3 Some words used to describe the fox are straightforward facts, whereas others are used by the writer to create emotions such as anger and disgust in the reader. Organise the following words into two lists to show which are factual and which are emotive.
   - razor-sharp teeth
   - animal
   - fox
   - plunged
   - creeping
   - beast

4 Rewrite paragraph 2 so that it is less emotive. Decide which words to change and which words to leave out so that the paragraph becomes more factual and less emotive. Show your new paragraph to a partner.

Text organisation

A newspaper article has to be organised in a way that makes the story clear to readers but also grabs their attention. Look closely at the way the article on page 83 is set out and answer these questions:

Activity 3

1 Why do you think the story is written in very short paragraphs?

2 What is the purpose of paragraphs 1–4?

3 How does the direction of the story change in paragraphs 8–10?

4 What are paragraphs 5–7 in the middle of the story about?

5 Look at the headline, sub-headline and paragraphs 1–3 again. What has the journalist done to grab the reader's attention? Think about:
- use of emotive language
- use of repetition
- how questions are raised in the reader's mind which make them want to read on.

6 Often a newspaper has to change the space it has allocated to one story quickly because other stories come in. If you needed to cut the story about Jessica and the fox, which lines would you delete so that the story still makes sense and has an impact. Think about:
- Which lines or sentences make the story especially interesting?
- Would the sense of the article be muddled by deleting certain paragraphs? For example, if paragraph 3 is deleted, how does that affect the beginning of paragraph 4?
- Are some paragraphs less important to the main story than others?

7 When you have finished, explain your decisions to a partner.

Feedback

Work with a partner to produce an annotated version of the article. Write notes to explain the following features of a newspaper article:

- how headlines are made effective
- how photographs add to the meaning of the words
- how and why articles are broken down into short paragraphs
- how the writer begins the article to grab the reader's attention
- how emotive language is used to create effect
- how quotations are used.

When you have finished, swap your annotated article with another pair of students. Check that they have effectively annotated the article with the five bullet points. Do the annotations give clear explanations? Use anything you learn from their annotations to improve your own.

Progress check

Below is a list of the main features of newspaper articles that you have explored so far. Write out the points below, then look back at the work you have done and give them 1–3 ticks, according to how you feel about your understanding of them:

- The difference between past and present tense.
- The reasons for writers of newspaper articles using the present tense when writing about things that happened in the past.
- Identifying emotive language and exploring its effects in newspaper articles.
- How quotations are used in newspaper articles.
- How paragraphs are organised and sequenced in newspaper articles.

1 tick = most confident
3 ticks = least confident.

Writing a formal letter

Because newspapers are read by a wide public, they are usually written in formal rather than informal language. Similarly, if you want to write an official letter, you would usually use formal language and follow established rules or conventions. Activity 4 explores some of the differences between formal and informal language in letters.

Activity 4

1 If you were an official working for the Council, how might you react to the letter on the right?

2 Think about the following features of the letter and briefly explain why they might mean that this letter is ignored:
- the lack of an address
- the way the receiver of the letter is addressed
- the presentation of the letter.

> Dear whoever you are,
>
> I'm right cheesed off with bins overflowing and rubbish all over the place. It's a health hazard. My little girl cut her knee on some broken glass last week and I've just about had enough. The lass next door said she saw a rat running around her bins. I fork out my council tax and I've had enough.
>
> An angry resident

3 Find two examples of slang and comment on whether you think it is appropriate for the writer to use informal language in this way. Think about the audience and purpose of this letter.

4 Read the letter below and the annotations, which draw attention to the features that make it a formal letter. Why might this letter be more likely to get a reply?

12 Antrobus Street — The address of the sender.
Mulverton
Hensham Spa
HE32 6EF

The date. It is always important to include the date for information, so that the receiver knows when it was sent. — 1 March 2005

Dear Sir/Madam, — This is a formal, respectful way to address someone in an official letter when you do not know their name.

The opening paragraph states the reason for writing. — I am writing to express my concern about some problems caused by the presence of large amounts of rubbish in Dark Lane, which is behind the street where I live.

The middle paragraph adds some more detail. — Considerable amounts of rubbish have been left uncollected for some weeks and this is clearly creating an unhealthy and dangerous environment. Whilst she was out playing, my own daughter cut her knee on some broken glass. Furthermore, rats have been seen in and around the rubbish.

Formal language used to create a polite tone.

The final paragraph states the writer's feelings and indicates what she would like to be done about the problem. — As a council-tax paying resident of Hensham Spa, I feel I am entitled to a better service than the one currently being provided. I would very much like to hear from you about what you can do to improve the situation.

Yours faithfully, — This is the formal way to end a letter to someone whose name you have not used at the start. If the letter had started, 'Dear Mr Brown…', it should end 'Yours sincerely'.

R. Mackin

Mrs R. Mackin

5 Write a letter to Islington Council about the foxes next door to Mr Brown. Look back at the letter on page 88 to help you.

Success criteria

To follow the conventions of formal letter-writing, you need to include the following.

☆ your address and date
☆ formal beginning 'Dear …'
☆ sentence explaining your reason for writing
☆ statement of what you want to happen next
☆ formal language throughout your letter
☆ formal ending.

 Sharpen spelling

Adding -ly

The word 'sincerely' is often spelled incorrectly. When a word ends in 'e' and you wish to add the suffix 'ly', you keep the 'e'. Another example of this is:

absolute → absolutely

Find and write down five other words ending in 'e' to which the suffix 'ly' can be added.

Feedback

When you have written your first draft, show your letter to a partner. Ask them to check that you have included all the success criteria listed above.

If you have missed any out, make alterations to your letter before you write the final draft.

After you have finished your letter, complete this sentence:

I think my letter will be successful in getting a reply because …

Linking paragraphs

As you have seen from the newspaper article and the formal letter, it is easier to read a text when it is written in paragraphs. It is also easier to read a text if every paragraph follows on logically from the one before it.

For example, look at the following four paragraphs from the newspaper article about the urban fox. The order has been changed from the original. Each paragraph on its own makes sense, but can you explain why paragraphs 3 and 4 do not link well in this version?

1 A girl of four was left in agony after being attacked by a fox as she slept in her bed.

2 Her panic-stricken parents Richard Brown and his wife, Corinne Magnier, both 36, had been watching TV when they heard her screams.

3 The animal plunged its razor-sharp teeth into Jessica Brown's arm after creeping through an open door at her home.

4 They rushed up to the bedroom and chased the fox out of their home in Tufnell Park, north London. They believe the animal was attracted by the smell of chicken the family had eaten earlier.

Activity 5

1 Here is another text from a newspaper. It consists of a headline and five paragraphs. The order of the paragraphs has been changed. Read them and put them in the correct order.

A *Life* has five pairs of tickets to give away to screenings between Monday, May 31, and Wednesday, June 2. To claim a pair, simply take this paper to a cashier at Stockport's UGC Cinema and show this page.

B The film stars Dennis Quaid, Ian Holm and Jake Gyllenhaal, in the year's biggest disaster film. Full of special effects, it tells the tale of what could happen to the world if global warming continued at high levels, resulting in catastrophe.

C Disaster film reigns at flicks this week

D Quaid plays Professor Adrian Hall, a scientist who tries to save the world from the effects of global warming, as well as trying to reach his son, Sam (Gyllenhaal), in New York – who sees the chilling effects of a new Ice Age first-hand.

A ROLAND EMMERICH FILM

THE DAY AFTER TOMORROW

12A CONTAINS EXTENDED SCENES OF PERIL

E Tickets MUST be collected on Monday, May 31, ONLY and will be allocated on a first come, first-served basis. Only one pair per couple and the manager's decision is final.

TWENTIETH CENTURY FOX PRESENTS A CENTROPOLIS ENTERTAINMENT/LIONS GATE/MARK GORDON COMPANY PRODUCTION A ROLAND EMMERICH FILM
"THE DAY AFTER TOMORROW" DENNIS QUAID J
FILM EDITOR DAVID BRENNER, A.C.E. PRODUCTION DESIGNER BARRY CHUSID
ROLAND EMMERICH STORY BY ROLAN

PREPARE to take cover at the cinema as the disaster movie returns with a bang. Stockport's UGC Cinema in the Grand Central leisure complex is giving away tickets to see 'The Day After Tomorrow' (cert 12A – contains extended scenes of peril).

©2004 TWENTIETH CENTURY FOX

2 When you are satisfied that you have the paragraphs in the right order, jot down some notes which explain, paragraph by paragraph, the clues that helped you work out the proper position of the paragraphs. For example, 'The film stars …' must follow a paragraph in which the name of the film is given.

Linking sentences within paragraphs

Just as it is easier to read a text if every paragraph follows on logically from the one before it, it is also easier to read a text if every sentence connects fluently with the one before it.

In paragraph A, notice how the words at the start of the second sentence link with the first sentence in the paragraph:
'To claim a pair' only makes sense if the reader knows what 'pair' is being referred to – and that information is given in the first sentence.

Highlight thinking

Sequential thinking
You use **sequential** thinking when you follow steps or ideas in a logical order. In English, this sort of thinking helps you to:

- put your own ideas and writing in an effective order
- recognise and analyse order and structure in the writing of others.

You also use sequential thinking in other subject areas too, for example:

- Maths – to work out the stages of a problem
- Science – to set up and write about experiments
- ICT – using software; programming.

Activity 6

Copy the sentences below and add some words which could be placed at the start of the second sentence to link the pairs of sentences. Write your linking words in a different colour and avoid using 'and'.

> Here is an example:
> He had an exam in the morning.   He went to bed early.
> He had an exam in the morning.   Realising its importance, he went to bed early.

a He watched his favourite programme on the television. He went to bed.
b The weather was beautifully warm and sunny. They had a picnic.
c The police officer approached the drunken man. He decided to arrest him.
d He placed the ball on the penalty spot. The crowd went quiet.

The organisation of leaflets

Like newspaper articles, information leaflets use a variety of presentational and organisational features to help readers find the information they need and to present the text in an attractive way.

Activity 7

Look at the leaflet on the opposite page for the tourist attraction of the village of Castleton.

1 Compare the presentation of information in this leaflet with the newspaper article about the fox on page 83. Look closely at the way each text is set out. Make a list of the similarities and differences you find. You might begin:
   Both use photographs.

2 What are the purposes of the seven photographs in the leaflet?

3 The leaflet is organised into two columns so that it can be folded, but the first paragraph of writing goes across both columns. Why do you think the designer of the leaflet has done that?

4 What 'messages' about Castleton are given by the logo in the top left of the leaflet?

5 The writer has arranged information about Castleton into six paragraphs. Each paragraph is about a slightly different aspect. It may be possible to change the order of the paragraphs and keep the sense, but there are reasons for the ways the paragraphs are grouped.
   a What kinds of information connect paragraphs 2, 3 and 4?
   b How is the information in paragraphs 5 and 6 different from that in the previous paragraphs?
   c Paragraph 6 begins with a connective: 'And'. What does 'And underground' connect with in the previous paragraph?

6 In paragraphs 4, 5 and 6, which have two sentences, the writer uses words at the start of the second sentence which link it to the first sentence. For example, in paragraph 6:

> And underground an equally impressive landscape emerges. Visitors can take trips down four very different show caves, Treak Cliff, Blue John, Speedwell and Peak.

These words link with the reference to an underground landscape in the first sentence.

Copy out paragraphs 4 and 5. Highlight words in the second sentence that link it to the first sentence.

CASTLETON

Nestling in the heart of the Peak National Park, Castleton is one of Britain's most fascinating villages and, however you approach, you will be struck by the magnificence of its location.

No wonder we call it 'The Gem of the Peaks.' It would be hard to imagine anywhere with such an array of natural and historical features both above and below ground.

The village of Castleton takes its name from the imposing ruins of Peveril Castle on the hillside above.

The spectacular Winnats Pass climbs 1300 feet out of the village, banked by near vertical cliffs. Overlooking the pass is Mam Tor, the name means "mother mountain" but it is known locally as "The Shivering Mountain" as its layers of gritstone and shale gradually crumble to cause landslips.

A walk up the old main road to see nature's power at work is worth the effort. You will also pass the remains of Odin Lead Mine with the crushing circle stone still in position.

And underground an equally impressive landscape emerges. Visitors can take trips down four very different show caves, Treak Cliff, Blue John, Speedwell and Peak.

PEAK CAVERN

SPEEDWELL CAVERN

BLUE JOHN CAVERN

Textbooks

Now you are going to look at the organisation of texts you will be very familiar with – your school textbooks. Different subjects use their own specific vocabulary and text organisation. For example, your Science textbooks will look very different from your English textbooks.

Make a list of the ways in which a Science textbook is different from an English textbook. Think about the text as well as the illustrations.

Activity 8

Read the text below, which is a set of instructions from a textbook, and answer the questions.

Sharpen spelling

Applying spelling rules

You probably know the rule 'i' before 'e' except after 'c' when the sound is *ee* as in *cheese*. For example: *believe*, *niece*. Here 'i' comes before 'e'. In *ceiling* and *receive* the rule works because the vowels make the sound *ee*, but 'e' comes before 'i' because they follow 'c'.

In *reign* and *weight* the 'ei' vowel combination makes the sound *ay* as in *plate*. In this example 'e' comes before 'i'.

Copy the words below and use the rules above to help you complete them with *ie* or *ei*.

| ach__ve | shr__k | rec__pt | misch__ |
| conc__ve | v__l | fr__ght | n__ghbour |

1 This word gives you a clue to the subject being taught in this text. What is the subject? How many more examples of specialised vocabulary can you find?

2 Why do you think this paragraph and the one above are short? Remember the purpose of this text is to instruct.

3 How is punctuation used to organise this sentence?

4 Why is a diagram used here?

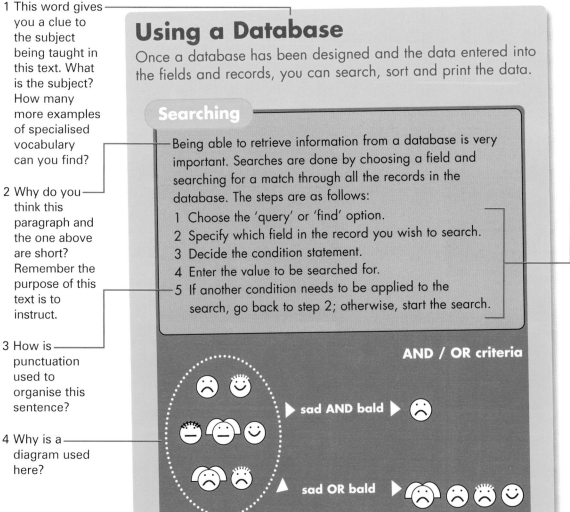

Using a Database

Once a database has been designed and the data entered into the fields and records, you can search, sort and print the data.

Searching

Being able to retrieve information from a database is very important. Searches are done by choosing a field and searching for a match through all the records in the database. The steps are as follows:

1 Choose the 'query' or 'find' option.
2 Specify which field in the record you wish to search.
3 Decide the condition statement.
4 Enter the value to be searched for.
5 If another condition needs to be applied to the search, go back to step 2; otherwise, start the search.

AND / OR criteria

▶ sad AND bald ▶

▲ sad OR bald ▶

5 Why is the information presented in list form with numbers?

6 Why do the sentences in this list use imperatives (commands)?

7 How well do you think this text has achieved its purpose of giving instructions? Give reasons for your answer.

Activity 9

Work with a partner to write a set of instructions on something you are an expert on, for example:

- importing an image into a document on a computer
- setting the video recorder
- riding a bike.

Your purpose is to give clear instructions which can be followed easily. Your audience is Year 7 students. Use the success criteria on the right to help you write clear and effective instructions.

Success criteria

- ☆ Write an introductory sentence.
- ☆ Use bullet points or number the points to separate the stages of the instructions.
- ☆ Use punctuation correctly to help readers understand your instructions easily.
- ☆ Use imperatives to give clear instructions to your readers.
- ☆ Use specialist vocabulary where necessary.

 Feedback

When you have written your instructions, show them to another pair of students and ask them to check your work using the success criteria above.

They should award you:

 A bronze medal if one or more stages of your instructions needs to be clearer.

 A silver medal if your instructions met most of the criteria

 A gold medal if your instructions met the criteria completely

If you get a bronze or silver medal, ask your partners to explain why, and then write one sentence beginning like this: To improve our instructions we need to . . .

Studying a text closely

Look closely at this extract from a History textbook, which is organised very differently from an instruction text. One of its purposes is to inform.

 ## Activity 10

1 Look back at the text about databases on page 94. Compare its layout with that of the text on page 96.
What do you notice about the way the two texts are presented on the page? What is similar about the layout and what is different? Think about:
- the use of colour
- the way the information is set out
- the use of headings and illustrations.

2 Now read the text closely and answer the questions on the right.

4.1 SEIZING CONTROL: HOW ROME BECAME AN EMPIRE

The Republic

Senate

600 influential citizens of Rome who advised the Consuls. They were very powerful, and ended up controlling Rome.

Consuls

Two Consuls governed Rome. They also commanded the army.

Tribunes

Protected the rights of the peasants – could block action by Senate or Consuls.

Assembly

Where the citizens of Rome met every year to elect the Consuls and Tribunes.

CiTizeNS of Rome are divided into two groups.

Wealthy citizens who often became Consuls or members of the Senate.

Patricians

Poorer citizens who disliked the Patricians having more power than them.

Plebeians

WoMen and Slaves were not allowed to Vote.

Rome was ruled by kings until 509 BC. After that Rome was a Republic – a state without a king or president. This is how the Republic worked.

The Republic breaks down

Until about 100 BC the Consuls only called up men to fight in the army when they needed them. **After** 100 BC Rome had a professional army of full-time soldiers. Some people were worried, quite rightly, that the army might decide to take over the city. In 87 BC General Gaius Marius did just that. He killed anyone against whom he had the slightest grudge. **Just a few years later** another general, Lucius Sulla, captured the city and made himself dictator. But perhaps the most famous of all the generals who seized power in Rome was Julius Caesar.

Caesar came from a leading Roman family. He was a brave soldier and in 59 BC was elected consul. After his year in office he was put in charge of the Roman army in Gaul. After seven years Caesar defeated all the tribes of Gaul.

Caesar's success made him enemies in Rome. One of these was General Pompey. Soon Pompey and Caesar were involved in a civil war to see who would control Rome. Caesar won and was made 'Dictator for life'. His head began to appear on coins. This was an honour usually reserved for the gods or dead officials. Many of the Senators decided the time had come to get rid of Caesar.

From *Living through History: The Roman Empire*

a Why do you think the writers chose to begin this section of the history book with pictures rather than continuous text?

b What specialist vocabulary is used here?

c If you were the reader of this text, how useful would you find this introduction? Give reasons for your answer.

d The words in bold are known as **temporal connectives**. They are words which link the sentences and paragraphs in a text by making reference to time. Why would you expect to find words like this in a history text?

e How many more temporal connectives can you find in the rest of the text?

3 The ideas in the history text on page 96 are organised in paragraphs. The purpose of a paragraph is to divide up the information so that readers can absorb it easily.

   a Read the text again and write one sentence to sum up the main point of each paragraph.

   b Headings are sometimes used in textbooks to sum up the main point of a paragraph. Decide on a heading for each of the last two paragraphs.

Comparing texts

Sometimes texts on the same topic can be presented very differently according to their audience and purpose.

Activity 11

1 Read Texts A and B on pages 98 and 99. Copy and complete the table below, using examples from the texts or your own comments.

	Text A	Text B
How headline appeals to or informs reader		
Organisation of sentences		
Serious/formal tone		
Lighthearted/informal tone		
Use of illustrations		

2 a With a partner, discuss statements 1–6 below and decide what you think about each one. Copy them out and record your decisions next to each one by writing:

   A   agree

   D   disagree

   N   not sure.

    1 Text A is a serious science text.

    2 Text B is also a serious science text.

    3 The illustrations in Text B do not help the reader to understand scientific information.

    4 Text A provides more information about the scientist and his work than Text B.

    5 Text B is more interesting to read.

    6 Text B has been written only to entertain.

b Discuss your opinions with another pair of students and explain to them why you made your choices.

c With a partner, discuss the advantages and disadvantages of each text. Which text gives you a clearer idea of the scientist's work in curing and preventing disease?

3 Use your answers to question 2 and evidence from the table to work out the audience and purpose of each text. Explain why you think each text was written and who the audience for each text is likely to be.

Text A

5.1 Great medical breakthroughs

Treating and preventing disease

Over the past 400 years many medical discoveries have been made. Because of these we are now able to cure or prevent many diseases which used to kill people.

Alexander Fleming made one of the greatest medical breakthroughs by chance in 1928. Fleming was studying bacteria and noticed that mould growing on an agar plate stopped a particular type of bacterium from growing. He grew more of the mould and obtained a substance from the broth called penicillin. He found it could destroy a number of different bacteria. In 1941, Howard Florey and Ernst Chain found a way of making penicillin in large amounts to use as a medicine.

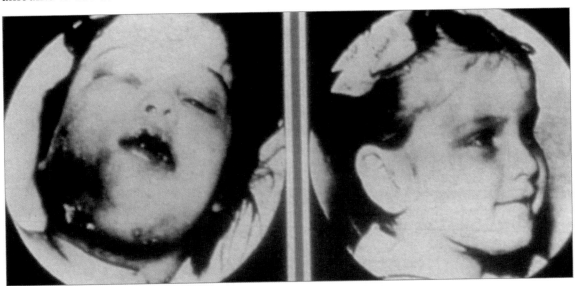

The first child to be treated with penicillin. Four weeks after treatment the infection was gone.

From *Eureka! 3R*

Text B

HORRIBLE SCIENCE HALL OF FAME:

LOUIS PASTEUR (1822-1895)
NATIONALITY: FRENCH

Louis Pasteur had embarrassing table manners. He would fiddle with his bread. He'd tear a slice into crumbs and inspect them for dust and wool and bits of cockroaches. If he found anything suspicious he would examine it at the table using a portable microscope. (Don't start getting ideas now!)

LOUIS PASTEUR WAS THE DEADLIEST ENEMY THE GERM WORLD EVER HAD. HE HUNTED GERMS LIKE A DETERMINED COP HUNTS A MASTER CRIMINAL. WITH A TOTAL AND RUTHLESS DEDICATION HE WORKED WEEKENDS AND EVENINGS – REFUSING TO GIVE UP EVER.

Here is just one of his achievements:

- He went on holiday leaving a mix of chicken cholera germs and broth. When he got back he found that many of the germs had died. He gave the mixture of weakened germs to some chickens and found they stayed healthy. The chickens' bodies had produced chemical defences against the dead germs that they could use to fight living germs. We call the dead germs a vaccine and it's what you get when you're vaccinated against a disease.

💬 Sharpen punctuation

Dashes

The text above uses a dash, for example:

> he worked weekends and evenings – refusing to give up ever

Sometimes in informal writing a dash is used where a comma or semi-colon would be used in more formal writing. In both cases, the effect is to create a pause.

Look at the following sentences and rewrite them using a dash to create a pause.

- Your teeth have a crushing power of 227kg (500 lbs) that's the weight of three men!
- Would you want to make yourself sick? Laz did in the interests of science umpteen times.

From *Disgusting digestion* by Nick Arnold

Activity 12

1 Read the text and answer the questions to help you work out how the writer entertains his readers.

A HORRIBLY HEALTHY DIET

There's a lot more to food than meets the eye. There are loads of vital ingredients that you must have in your daily diet. To find out more we persuaded Private Eye M.I. Gutzache to sneak back into the school kitchens to collect samples. At first he said he couldn't face going back to that revolting place. But after a bit of bribery and gentle persuasion with a roll of banknotes he dragged himself off his sick bed.

SAMPLE 2 – A GLASS OF WATER

It wasn't much to look at, but my investigation revealed that you need about two litres (3.5 pints) of this clear runny stuff every day. Half of this comes from water in your food (like the watery potato), and half from what you actually drink. You've got to top up your water supply 'cos your body is two-thirds water and bits such as your brain are 80 per cent water. So you know what'll happen if you don't drink enough of it – pea-brain!

a What has the writer done in this text to make the topic of a healthy diet interesting and entertaining to readers?

b Explain why the writer has chosen this name.

c Why do you think the writer uses the word revolting?

d In what way does the illustration make links with the text?

e Why does the writer address his readers as pea-brain?

From *Disgusting digestion* by Nick Arnold

2 The style of this text is different from that of a traditional science textbook. It sounds as if the writer is talking directly to his readers.

Write down three examples from the text where the writer addresses the reader directly.

3 Find and write down three examples where the writer has used humour to entertain his readers.

Writing your own text to entertain

You are going to write your own short text about one of the subjects you study in school. Your audience is young people of your own age, so you will need to use informal language. Your purpose is to entertain your readers.

> **Success criteria**
>
> The success criteria for this piece of writing are:
> ☆ using humour to entertain your readers.
> ☆ speaking directly to your readers, for example by asking them questions or using the second person pronoun *you* to help them relate to your text
> ☆ using an informal, conversational tone.

Follow these steps:

Step 1 Choose your subject
Think of a subject you could write about in an entertaining and humorous way.
I have chosen ... because ...

Step 2 Plan what you want to say
Make a list of things you want to say about your subject. These could be:
- things you find difficult or enjoyable about the subject
- things you have to do when studying your subject, such as lots of calculations or pages of writing
- any jokes you know or could make up about your subject.

Write down your ideas for illustrations.

Step 3 Write the first draft
Write your first draft (8 to 10 lines) and include the following:
- humour
- a statement of your own opinion
- direct address to your readers using the pronoun *you*
- dashes to replace some commas
- informal style and language
- questions which address your readers directly
- examples your readers can relate to
- illustrations
- your own comments.

Step 4 Get feedback
1 Show your first draft to a partner. Ask them to tick your work where you have included each of the items on the list in Step 3 above.

2 You should have 9 ticks. If you have fewer than this, ask your partner to show where you could include the features you have missed out.

Step 5 Write the final version
Once you have made all the improvements suggested by your partner, write the final version.

◯ Making notes

Before you start a piece of writing, you need to think and plan. Sometimes planning includes making notes. You also need to make notes when you are researching a topic or revising for an exam.

When you make notes you identify the key points in a text and write them down. Notes are always brief and never written in full sentences.

Activity 13

In this activity you will explore three different ways of making notes.

1 Read the following text and study the model notes on it, which have been made by three students from the same class. Work with a partner to answer the questions after each set of notes.

2 With your partner, list the advantages and disadvantages of each of the three models.

3 Which of the three models would you prefer to use? Explain why.

> **Word bank**
>
> **genera** family
> **tendril** a special leaf used by climbing plants to attach themselves to a support
> **peristome** area around the mouth of the leaves

Carnivorous Plants
Pitcher plants

Pitcher plants capture their prey by means of modified, cup-shaped leaves or 'pitchers' which contain digestive fluid.

Insects are induced to land inside the pitcher where they lose their footing, fall into the pool of fluid below and drown.

The traps vary considerably in size and construction. In the genera *Sarracenia* and *Heliamphora*, for example, they are 10 to 60 cm (4 to 24 in) long and are formed from a whole leaf, whereas in *Nepenthes* and *Cephalotus* they are 5 to 40 cm (2 to 16 in) long and are formed by a tendril-like growth from the leaf tip.

To attract insects, the rim and the inner wall of the pitcher are often a bright red colour, and many pitchers secrete a viscous sugary fluid on to the peristome and the underside of the lid as an added attraction.

Model 1

Pitcher Plants

What are they?	How do they trap insects?	How do insects die?
* plts with special leaves	* traps diff. sizes	* land in pitcher
* shaped like cups	* whole leaf/tendril	* fall into fluid
* trap ins.	* ins. attracted by colour/sugary fluid	* drown

a Why has this student used a chart for the notes?

b Why has the student shortened some of the words? What do the abbreviations stand for?

c Why has the student used different headings?

Model 2

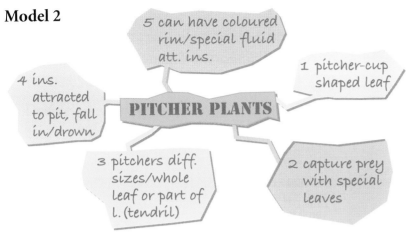

5 can have coloured rim/special fluid att. ins.

1 pitcher-cup shaped leaf

4 ins. attracted to pit, fall in/drown

PITCHER PLANTS

3 pitchers diff. sizes/whole leaf or part of l. (tendril)

2 capture prey with special leaves

a Do these notes cover the same information as Model 1 on page 102?

b How will the numbers help the student to organise his/her work?

Model 3

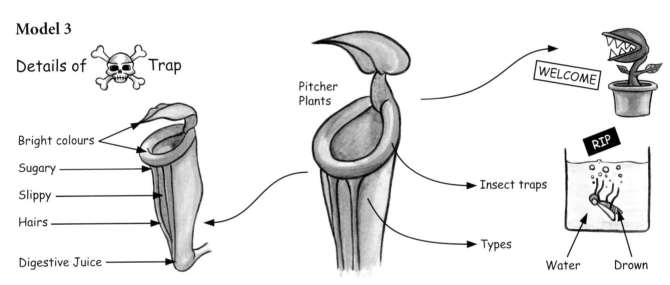

Details of ☠ Trap

Bright colours

Sugary

Slippy

Hairs

Digestive Juice

Pitcher Plants

WELCOME

Insect traps

Types

RIP

Water   Drown

a Why has the student included pictures as well as words?

b This model does not use numbers or chart headings. How has the writer organised his/her notes?

Activity 14

The students who made the notes above have made them brief and to the point. They have done this in two ways: by shortening sentences and shortening words.

In Model 1 the sentence 'Insects are induced to land inside the pitcher where they lose their footing, fall into the pool of fluid below and drown' becomes:

- fall into pitcher
- drown in fluid.

1 Look closely at the original. Which types of words has the student missed out to reduce the full sentence to two short phrases?

Highlight thinking

Mindmapping

Mindmapping can be used for **creative thinking** (coming up with ideas) and **critical thinking** (analysing ideas). Mindmaps take ideas further than spider diagrams and brainstorms, because you can extend the branches. Mindmaps also often use colour and pictures. These help get more of your brain working, and so help you to learn.

2 Model 2 uses these shortened words: *diff.*, *plts.* and *ins.*

    a What are each of these words when written in full?

    b Which part of the word has been missed out to create the shortened words?

3 Write your own abbreviations for these words:

- capture
- digestive
- pitcher
- sugary.

 Progress check

  1 Design a revision sheet to summarise what you have learned about note-taking. Include:
- why you need to take notes
- why notes should be brief
- how you can shorten words and sentences when making notes.

  2 Compare your sheet with a partner's. Do both of your revision sheets say the same things or have you missed something out? If so, make any necessary changes.

Making your own notes

You are going to read a text about the Battle of Hastings and make your own notes on the key points. You will then use your notes to write two paragraphs for a history book called *Battles in Brief*. Your audience is students of your own age. Your purpose is to inform.

> **Success criteria**
>
> ☆ Include all the key facts.
> ☆ Use formal language suited to a school textbook.
> ☆ Use temporal connectives (such as *next*, *afterwards*) to make the order of events clear.

Remember:
- notes should be brief
- you should shorten words and miss out unimportant words
- you can use numbers, pictures, tables or headings to help you organise your ideas.

Activity 15

1 Read the text opposite and think about the key points you will need to keep, such as the main events in the battle and what happened to the people involved. Think carefully about the facts you want to miss out as well as those you want to include. Then make your notes.

2 Use your notes to write two paragraphs on the Battle of Hastings which explain the events clearly. You should write in standard English and use a formal style.

  a Write your first draft using the success criteria to help you.

  b Read your first draft and make notes on the improvements you could make. Use the success criteria to help you.

  c Show your revised draft to another student and ask them to:

  • annotate your work to show where you have used temporal connectives

  • underline five key facts in your account

  • highlight two places where you have used formal language

  • advise you about changes you should make.

  d Make the changes suggested by your partner and then write the final version.

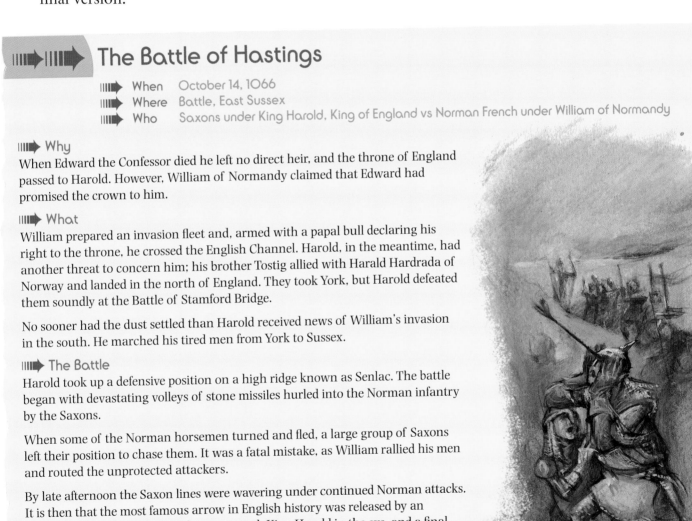

The Battle of Hastings

➤ **When** October 14, 1066
➤ **Where** Battle, East Sussex
➤ **Who** Saxons under King Harold, King of England vs Norman French under William of Normandy

➤ **Why**
When Edward the Confessor died he left no direct heir, and the throne of England passed to Harold. However, William of Normandy claimed that Edward had promised the crown to him.

➤ **What**
William prepared an invasion fleet and, armed with a papal bull declaring his right to the throne, he crossed the English Channel. Harold, in the meantime, had another threat to concern him; his brother Tostig allied with Harald Hardrada of Norway and landed in the north of England. They took York, but Harold defeated them soundly at the Battle of Stamford Bridge.

No sooner had the dust settled than Harold received news of William's invasion in the south. He marched his tired men from York to Sussex.

➤ **The Battle**
Harold took up a defensive position on a high ridge known as Senlac. The battle began with devastating volleys of stone missiles hurled into the Norman infantry by the Saxons.

When some of the Norman horsemen turned and fled, a large group of Saxons left their position to chase them. It was a fatal mistake, as William rallied his men and routed the unprotected attackers.

By late afternoon the Saxon lines were wavering under continued Norman attacks. It is then that the most famous arrow in English history was released by an anonymous Norman archer. The arrow took King Harold in the eye, and a final Norman onslaught killed him where he stood. The day belonged to Duke William, soon to be dubbed 'the Conqueror'.

Assessment task

> ### Writing a biography of a famous person
>
> A biography is an account of someone's life. You are going to research a famous person and then write a short biography about them. Your biography will be included in a book called *Lives of Famous People*.

You should write five paragraphs (maximum 250 words). In your piece of writing, you should:

- provide a range of information to interest people of your own age
- help readers find and digest the information easily
- design and present your text attractively.

You will use some of the skills you have been developing throughout this unit. The key skills are:

- organising writing into paragraphs
- effective note-taking
- linking paragraphs and sentences
- using presentational devices, such as fonts, pictures, etc.

Follow Steps 1–4 below and on page 107:

Step 1 Choose your famous person

Choose a famous person, who may be living or dead.

Step 2 Make a plan

Before you start researching your famous person, use what you know about them already to plan a framework of five paragraphs. For example, if you were researching William Shakespeare, you might decide something like this:

Paragraph 1: an introduction stating Shakespeare's main claim to fame
Paragraph 2: something about his early life before he became famous
Paragraph 3: his early life in the theatre
Paragraph 4: his major achievements
Paragraph 5: why he remains famous.

If you don't plan like this, you might end up reading a lot without really knowing what you are looking for. Of course, you might change your mind about your framework when you start your research.

Step 3 Do your research and make notes

Now you are ready to start your research. To find the information you need, you could search:

- the Internet
- books from a library
- newspapers and magazines.

When you find information that suits your needs, make your own copy of it. You shouldn't copy out large chunks from a book or cut and paste from the Internet – use the note-making skills you developed on pages 102–5. Remember that you have a maximum of 250 words, and you have to write five paragraphs, so don't be over ambitious.

Step 4 Start writing

Use the skills you have explored in this unit.

- Organise your information into paragraphs.
- Link paragraphs and sentences within paragraphs.

As you are writing, check your work with a partner, read your partner's work and make suggestions about how any parts of the work might be improved. For example:

- Does each paragraph concentrate on a different aspect of the famous person's life?
- Are the paragraphs in a logical order?
- In each paragraph, do the sentences flow into each other and are they in a logical order?
- Has the writer made any attempt to link each paragraph to the one before?

If the answer to any of these questions is 'no', help him or her put things right.

Step 5 Evaluate your writing

When you have finished your biography, evaluate it against the key skills list on page 106. Select one of these sentences to complete that best describes your biography:

I was very satisfied with my biography because …

I was quite satisfied but I still need to work on the following skills …

I was not happy with my biography because …

Highlight thinking

Critical thinking: research
Successful research involves good critical thinking. You have to find out key information, then sift through it and decide what is important to you. Good researchers must:

- decide which are the most useful sources for the project
- read through what they find and choose only the relevant and important information.

Research skills are important in a whole range of subjects – not just English.

5 Assessing evidence

The bigger picture

In this unit you will read a range of texts, both fiction and non-fiction. You will investigate how writers explore ideas and learn how to assess a range of information. At the end of the unit you will present a balanced analysis of an environmental issue.

WHAT? You will:
- investigate how an idea is explored by different writers
- examine how texts reflect the culture in which they were produced
- learn how to assess a range of evidence

HOW? by:
- reading different texts that explore the same idea
- reading texts from different cultures and identifying how they reflect place and time
- examining an issue and writing a balanced response to it

WHY? because:
- you develop reading skills by exploring connections between texts
- reading texts from different cultures helps you develop your understanding of other peoples and places
- you need to be able to understand and assess information in order to make sound judgements.

Exploring a theme

Different writers can explore the same theme in a range of ways. You are going to read three texts:

- an extract from a story
- a poem
- an extract from a non-fiction text.

You will then investigate what each writer has to say about the killing of whales.

The first extract is taken from a book, *The Whale Rider*, written by a New Zealand Maori. The Maoris were the people already living in New Zealand when it was explored by Captain Cook in 1769. In the book, the narrator recounts an incident when the men and boys were gathered in their meeting house and his niece Kahu overheard Koro Apirana's (Paka) story of whaling when he was younger.

A Maori meeting house

Working out the meaning of words

Texts often contain words that are special to a culture. Sometimes we can make a rough guess at their meaning based on clues in what comes before and after the word. This is called the **context**.

Read the first paragraph of the extract and try to work out what the Maori word 'Paikea' means.

> In the evening after our lesson on the sea we assembled in the meeting house. The booming on the open waters had heralded the coming of a rainstorm. As I went into the meeting house I glanced up at our
> 5 ancestor, <u>Paikea</u>. He looked like he was lifting his whale through the spearing rain.

Did you spot these clues?

Paikea – a capital letter is used so it's a name; 'ancestor' so it's a person; 'he' so it's a male. A picture in the meeting house suggests he was honoured. There's some connection with a whale.

Highlight thinking

Critical thinking: analysing

Analysis means a sort of investigation. You have to look for important factors in order to understand how something works or to come up with an answer. You are acting as a sort of detective, looking for important clues. You have to decide what is important and what is not, and decide on what is most likely, based on the evidence.

Analysis is important in English because it helps you to:

- explore the meaning of texts
- understand the ways in which writers use evidence.

When we look this word up in a Maori dictionary we find that Paikea was a famous Maori who, according to legend, rode a whale.

Activity 1

1 As you read the rest of the extract on page 111, try to work out the meaning of the Maori words, by looking for clues in the context. The Maori words are underlined. You may already know some of them.

2 When you have finished reading, copy and complete the table below. Aim to list as many clues as you can to help explain each word.

Word	Clues
Koro Apirana	Capital letters suggest it's a name 'led the prayer' suggests he is an important person
karakia	

 Feedback

1 Check your table with a partner's. Have you picked out the same clues? Are there any clues you have missed? Add them to your table.

2 Together, decide what each word means. Create a word bank for this extract.

3 Check your word bank with the word bank on page 132. For each word, award one mark if you came close to its meaning. If you got more than five marks, you have shown you can work out the meaning of words from clues in the context.

Koro Apirana led us in karakia, a prayer to bless the wananga. Then, after the mihimihi, he told us of the times which had brought the silence to the sea.

'I was a boy of seven years' age,' he began, 'when I went to stay with my uncle who was a whaler. I was too young to know any better, and I didn't understand
5 then, as I do now, about our tipua. At the time whaling was one of the great pastimes and once the bell on the lookout had been sounded you'd see all the whaling boats tearing out to sea, chasing after a whale. Doesn't matter what you were doing, you'd drop everything, your plough, your sheep clippers, your schoolbooks, *everything*. I can still remember seeing everyone climbing the
10 lookout, like white balloons. I followed them and far out to sea I saw a herd of whales.'

The rain fell through his words. 'They were the most beautiful sight I had ever seen.' He made a sweeping gesture. 'Then, down by the slipway, I could see the longboats being launched into the sea. I ran down past the sheds and the pots on
15 the fires were already being stoked to boil down the blubber. All of a sudden my uncle yelled out to me to get on his boat with him. So there I was, heading out to sea.'

I saw a spiky kina sneaking a look through the door.

'That's when I saw the whales really close,' Koro Apirana said. 'There must
20 have been sixty of them at least. I have never forgotten, never. They had mana. They were so powerful. Our longboat got so close to one that I was able to reach out and touch the skin.' His voice was hushed with awe. 'I felt the ripple of power beneath the skin. It felt like silk. Like a god. Then the harpoons began to sing through the air. But I was young, you see, and all I could feel was the thrill,
25 like when you do a haka.'

He paused, mesmerised. 'I can remember that when a whale was harpooned it would fight with all its strength. Eventually it would spout blood like a fountain, and the sea would be red. Three or four other boats would tow it ashore to the nearest place and cut it up and share out the meat and the oil and everything. When we
30 started to strip the blubber off the whale in the whaling station, all the blood flowed into the channel. Blind eels would come up with the tide to drink the blood.'

I heard Kahu weeping at the doorway. I edged over to her and when she saw me she put her arms around my neck.

'You better go home,' I whispered, 'before Koro Apirana finds out you're here.'

35 But she was so frightened. She was making a mewling sound in her throat. She seemed paralysed with terror.

Inside, Koro Apirana was saying, 'When it was all finished we would cut huge slabs of whale meat and sling them across our horses and take them to our homes –'

40 Suddenly, before I could stop her, Kahu wrenched away from me and ran into the meeting house.

'No, Paka, *no*!' she screamed.

His mouth dropped open. 'Haere atu koe,' he shouted.

'Paka. Paka, no!'

45 Grimly, Koro Apirana walked up to her, took her by the arms and virtually hurled her out. 'Haere atu. *Haere*,' he repeated. The sea thundered ominously. The rain fell like spears.

From *The Whale Rider* by Witi Ihimaera

Investigating culture

The word **culture** is a general term for the huge range of ideas, knowledge and beliefs that are generally shared by the people of a country or race. Throughout the extract above the writer refers to things that tell us about the Maori culture, for example:

- 'we assembled in the meeting house' – suggests that the people meet together often.
- there is an image of their ancestor, Paikea, in the meeting house – suggests they honour their famous ancestors.

These details help the reader build a picture of Maori culture.

Activity 2

What do each of the following details from the extract suggest to you about the Maori culture?

- 'Koro Apirana led us in karakia, a prayer to bless the wananga.'
- 'At the time whaling was one of the great pastimes.'
- 'Doesn't matter what you were doing, you'd drop everything, your plough, your sheep clippers, your schoolbooks, *everything*.'

Traditional Maori man

 How to refer to evidence in a text

- When you write about a text, you should refer to evidence in it to support the points you make. This evidence may be **details from the text**, for example:

  We know that Kahu is upset by what she has heard because she weeps and makes a strange sound.

- Sometimes you will want to quote directly from the text to provide the evidence. You might want to **quote single words or phrases**, for example:

  Koro Apirana says that when he was a boy whaling was thought to be 'one of the great pastimes'.

  Notice how quotation marks are placed directly before and after the words that are taken from the text.

Highlight thinking

Critical thinking: justifying

Justifying means giving reasons/ evidence to back up your points or ideas. For example, using evidence from the text to support your ideas about Maori culture.

Justifying is an important skill in English because it lets you:

- show how you have developed your ideas about a text
- explain your point of view in your own writing
- understand how other writers build an argument.

- Occasionally, you might want to **quote a whole sentence or more** as evidence for the point you want to make, for example:

  When describing the whale's skin, Koro Apirana says:
  'I felt the ripple of power beneath the skin. It felt like silk.
  Like a god.'

  Notice how a colon is used to show that a quotation is to follow and that the quotation starts on a new line when one or more whole sentences are being quoted.

Activity 3

Using what you learnt about the language in Activity 1 and the notes you made in Activity 2, write four or five sentences explaining what you have learnt about the Maori culture from this extract. Refer to details in the text and use quotations to justify the things you say.

Feedback

Check your writing against points 1–4 below.
1 Number the points you have made about the Maori culture.
  a Underline the details from the text you have referred to.
  b Underline the quotations from the text you have used.
  c Circle the quotation marks.

2 Is every point supported by evidence? If not, think about what evidence you could use and add it.

3 Have you used colons to introduce long quotations and started the quotation on a new line?

4 How confident do you feel about how to refer to evidence in a text? Copy the diagram below.

Colour the first row of blocks if you know how to refer to evidence without quoting.
Colour the second row if you know how to quote a whole sentence or more.
Colour the third row if you know how to quote words and phrases.

Identifying the writer's attitude

When we refer to a writer's attitude we mean the way he or she thinks and feels about certain things. You are going to explore how the writer of the extract on page 111 reveals his attitude through:

- what he writes
- how he writes.

Activity 4

1 The evidence in the second column of the table below supports the statements in the first column. Copy the table and find and list at least one more piece of evidence from the extract on page 111 for each statement.

Statement	Evidence
Koro Apirana regrets what has happened.	• 'I was too young to know any better' •
Whales are presented as creatures of beauty.	• 'They were the most beautiful sight I had ever seen' •
The killing of the whales is shown to be cruel.	• 'Eventually it [the whale] would spout blood like a fountain, and the sea would be red.' •
Kahu is disturbed by what she has heard.	• 'I heard Kahu weeping at the doorway.' •

2 Check your evidence with a partner and talk about:
- what you think is the writer's attitude to the killing of whales
- why you think this.

3 Write a paragraph explaining the writer's attitude to the killing of whales. Use evidence from the text to support the points you make. Remember to use quotation marks if you are using a direct quotation from the text.

Looking for implied meaning

It is not always easy to identify the attitude of the writer. Sometimes a writer is careful not to give too much away. The meaning may be hidden or implied rather than clearly stated. However, if you read closely, think carefully and ask the right questions you can usually work it out.

Read the poem on page 115 closely two or three times. Then answer the questions in Activity 5 on page 116.

Killing a Whale

A whale is killed as follows:
A shell is filled with dynamite and
A harpoon takes the shell.
You wait until the great grey back
5 **Breaches** the sliding seas, you squint,
Take aim.
The cable snakes like a squirt of paint,
The shell channels deep through **fluke**
And **flank**, through **mural** softness
10 To bang among the blubber,
Exploding terror through
The hollow fleshy chambers,
While the hooks fly open
Like an umbrella
15 Gripping the tender tissue.

It dies with some **panache**,
Whipping the **capstan** like
A schoolboy's wooden top,
Until the teeth of the machine
20 Can hold its anger, grip.
Its dead tons thresh for hours
The ravished sea,
Then sink together, sag –
So air is pumped inside
25 To keep the corpse afloat,
And one of those flags that men
Kill mountains with is stuck
Into this massive death.

Dead whales are rendered down,
30 Give oil.

David Gill

Word bank

breaches breaks clear of the water
fluke either of the two lobes of the tail of a whale
flank the side of the whale
mural the internal structure of the body of the whale
panache style
capstan a device used on ships for hauling in ropes

Activity 5

Answer these questions to help you identify the poet's attitude to whaling.

1 According to the first line of the poem, what is the poem going to be about?

2 Why do you think the poet uses the word 'you' twice in lines 4–5?

3 Which of the following words would you use to describe the tone of lines 1–6? Give reasons for your answer.
  - impersonal
  - calm
  - angry
  - indifferent

4 The poet tells us 'the cable snakes like a squirt of paint'. What different things are suggested by the use of the word 'snakes'?

5 Re-read lines 8–15. What words does the poet use to suggest this is:
   a a frightening experience for the whale   **b** a painful experience for the whale?

6 What simile is used in lines 17–18? How does this simile imply that the whale is a powerful creature?

7 The word 'corpse' usually refers to the dead body of a human. Why do you think the poet chose to use this word?

8 Why do men stick flags into mountains? What does the poet imply by using this comparison to describe the flag that is stuck into the whale?

9 The poem ends with a couplet. What do you think the poet is trying to make clear to the reader in these two lines?

Activity 6

1 Below are seven statements about the poet's attitude. For each one:

- find evidence from the poem that supports it
- explain how the evidence supports it.

a The poet is against the killing of whales.

b The poet shows that it is just a job.

c The poet is fascinated by the process of the killing.

d The poet thinks it is a painful death.

e The poet thinks men just want to show their power over whales.

f The poet is disgusted by the killing of whales.

g The poet thinks the oil from the whales is valuable.

2 Put the statements in order, placing the one you most agree with first and the one you least agree with last.

 Sharpen spelling

The 'y' sound

A -y in a word can act as a vowel. It can be pronounced in different ways.

1 Sort the following words into five groups where:

- the -y has the long -ie sound as in *fly*
- the -y has the short -i sound as in *gym*
- the -y has the long -ee sound as in *candy*
- the -y has the long -oi sound as in *boy*
- the -y has the short -ae sound as in *day*.

Some words may appear in more than one list!

dynamite	typist	typhoon
mystery	worry	crayon
style	alloy	hymn
system	gypsy	away
try	joyous	century
syrup	haywire	

2 In pairs, test yourselves on the spelling of the words in each of the three groups.

Recognising language differences

The ways ideas are expressed and written changes over time. The following extract about whaling was written more than one hundred years ago, in 1898. Read the first paragraph closely. The annotations show you some of the differences between this and modern English.

Before it was fairly light we lowered, and paddled as swiftly as possible to the bay where we had last seen the spout overnight. When near the spot we rested on our paddles a while,[1] all hands looking out with intense eagerness for the first sign of the whale's appearance. There was a strange feeling among us of
5 unlawfulness and stealth, as of ambushed pirates[2] waiting to attack some unwary merchantman[3], or highwaymen[3] waylaying a fat alderman[3] on a country road. We spoke in whispers, for the morning was so still that a voice raised but ordinarily would have reverberated among the rocks which almost overhung us,[4] multiplied indefinitely. A turtle rose ghost-like to the surface at my side, lifting his
10 queer head, and, surveying us with stony gaze, vanished as silently as he came.

1 We would say *for a while*

2 This is old-fashioned usage. We would say 'like ambushed pirates'.

3 This vocabulary is no longer in everyday use.

4 Use of long clauses makes the language seem very formal.

Activity 7

1 Read the rest of the extract.

2 Rewrite the highlighted phrases in modern English.

3 Explain what you needed to do in order to rewrite them.

One looked at the other inquiringly, but the repetition of that long expiration satisfied us all that it was the placid breathing of the whale we sought somewhere close at hand. There was a ripple just audible, and away glided the mate's boat right for the near shore. Following him with our eyes, we almost
15 immediately beheld a pale, shadowy column of white, shimmering against the dark mass of the cliff not a quarter of a mile away. Dipping our paddles with the utmost care, we made after the chief, almost holding our breath. The harpooner rose, darted once, twice, then gave a yell of triumph that ran re-echoing all around in a thousand eerie vibrations.

20 But, for all the notice taken by the whale, she might never have been touched. Close nestled to her side was a youngling of not more, certainly, than five days old, which sent up its baby-spout every now and then about two feet into the air. One long, wing-like fin embraced its small body, holding it close to the massive breast of the tender mother, whose only care seemed to be to protect her
25 young, utterly regardless of her own pain and danger. If sentiment were ever permitted to interfere with such operation as ours, it might well have done so now; for while the calf continually sought to escape from the enfolding fin, making all sorts of puny struggles in the attempt, the mother scarcely moved from her position, although streaming with blood from a score of wounds.

30 So in the most perfect quiet, with scarcely a writhe, nor any sign of flurry, she died, holding the calf to her side until her last vital spark had fled, and left it to a swift despatch with a single lance-thrust. No slaughter of a lamb ever looked more like murder. Nor, when the vast bulk and strength of the animal was considered, could a mightier example have been given of the force and quality
35 of maternal love.

> ### Word bank
> **expiration** the breathing out of air
> **writhe** to twist or squirm in pain

From *The Cruise of the 'Cachalot' Round the World after Sperm Whales* by Frank T. Bullen

Exploring the writer's comments

Writers often show their attitude through direct comments.

Activity 8

1 Re-read the following comments from the extract on pages 117–18. With a partner work out, and write down, what you think each comment shows about the writer's attitude to killing this whale.

> **A** There was a strange feeling among us of unlawfulness and stealth, as of ambushed pirates waiting to attack some unwary merchantman, or highwaymen waylaying a fat alderman on a country road. (lines 4–7)

> **B** If sentiment were ever permitted to interfere with such operation as ours, it might well have done so now; for while the calf continually sought to escape from the enfolding fin, making all sorts of puny struggles in the attempt, the mother scarcely moved from her position, although streaming with blood from a score of wounds. (lines 25–9)

> **C** No slaughter of a lamb ever looked more like murder. Nor, when the vast bulk and strength of the animal was considered, could a mightier example have been given of the force and quality of maternal love. (lines 32–5)

2 Think about the three comments together. What does the writer seem to be saying about:
- the killing of this whale
- the way he feels about this whale?

 Sharpen punctuation

Commas

Commas show us when to pause to make sense of a complex sentence. Read the following sentence aloud, pausing at each comma: 'A turtle rose ghost-like to the surface at my side, lifting his queer head, and, surveying us with stony gaze, vanished as silently as he came.'

1 With a partner, decide where the commas should come in the following sentences. Copy out the sentences and put the commas in. Do not look back at the extract.

> 'One long wing-like fin embraced its small body holding it close to the massive breast of the tender mother whose only care seemed to be to protect her young utterly regardless of her own pain and danger.'

2 Check your commas against the sentences in the passage on page 118. Did you put them in the same place as the writer? If not, why not?

✓ Progress check

You have examined the way the killing of whales is explored and presented by three different writers and have learnt how to refer to the text to support the points you make. Check your skills by reading the following text closely and answering the questions.

> In the water whales have become the dominant species,
> Without killing their own kind.
> In the water, whales have become the dominant species,
> Though they allow the resources they use to renew themselves.
> 5 In the water, whales have become the dominant species,
> Though they use language to communicate, rather than to eliminate rivals,
> In the water, whales have become the dominant species,
> Though they do not broodily guard their patch with bristling security.
> In the water, whales have become the dominant species,
> 10 Though they acknowledge minds other than their own.
> In the water, whales have become the dominant species,
> Without allowing their population to reach plague proportions.
>
> From space, the planet is blue.
> From space, the planet is the territory
> 15 Not of humans, but of the whale.

From *Whale Nation* by Heathcote Williams

1 Choose and write down two details which show that the writer has a high opinion of whales.

2 Lines 2, 4, 6, 8, 10 and 12 suggest something about humans as well as about the whale. What different things do these lines suggest about humans?

3 Use your answers to 1 and 2 to help you write two paragraphs.
   • In paragraph 1 explain the writer's attitude to the whale.
   • In paragraph 2 explain the writer's attitude to humans.
   In both paragraphs, refer to the text and use quotations to support the points you make.

4 Read a partner's paragraphs. Use the sentences below to show your opinion of *each* of the paragraphs. You may not actually agree with what they say, but remember that you are just assessing how well they have explained their views.
   • I think your (first/second) explanation is (clear/unclear) and (based/not based) on the text.
   • You (have/have not) used quotations to support the points you make.

5 Think about your partner's opinion. Can you improve your own paragraphs? If yes, rewrite your answers and make sure you refer to the text.

Weighing up the evidence

In this unit you have learnt how to:
- identify the attitude of the writer
- refer to the text to support the points you make.

Now you are going to examine a range of texts to help you answer a question. This is what you need to do when you are researching a subject.

Nessie, of Loch Ness in Scotland, is one of the most publicised and well known of lake monsters. There are hundreds of sightings on record over a period of 200 years. However, the existence of Nessie has never been proved and there are numerous theories to explain away the evidence.

On pages 122–6 you will find a wide range of texts about the Loch Ness Monster. To help you learn how to write a balanced response to a question, you will:
- sift through the texts to assess their usefulness
- ask questions about the texts to assess how reliable they are
- make notes on the texts you want to use
- examine a model answer to the question: **'Does Nessie exist?'**

Activity 9

Follow and complete these stages to help you prepare an answer to the question: **'Does Nessie exist?'**

Stage 1 Sift through the texts

The first thing you need to do is to decide which of the texts are going to be most useful to you in deciding whether there is a Loch Ness Monster. Skim-read Texts A–H on pages 122–6. Then copy out and complete the following table.

Text	What it is	What it's about	Its usefulness 0–3 and reason(s) for score
A	Table of recorded sightings	Examples of when the monster's been seen	3 – gives a range of evidence over many years

Stage 2 Question the texts

Not everything people say or write is true. To help you weigh up the usefulness of a text, you need to ask questions. On the next page are some questions you could ask about Text A:

- Do these sightings have anything in common?
- Why were none of these people carrying a camera?
- How could a recorded sighting of Nessie be of advantage to a hotel?
- Why are most of the sightings in the summer months?

Notice how, in order to ask good questions, you need to think outside the text. You need to act like a detective who is trying to uncover the truth.

With a partner, work out and write down the questions you would want to ask about Texts B and E.

Stage 3 Make notes
To help you to refer confidently to the evidence, make notes on four or five of the most useful texts. Your notes should:

- summarise the key points in the text
- ask the main questions that need to be asked
- be short, as there is no need to write in sentences and you can use abbreviations.

Stage 4 Group the evidence
Using your notes to help you, make two separate lists of:

- the evidence that suggests Nessie exists
- the evidence that suggests Nessie does not exist.

Text A

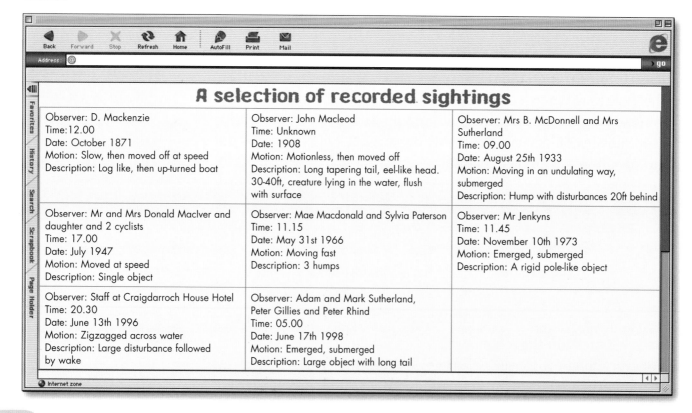

A selection of recorded sightings

Observer: D. Mackenzie Time: 12.00 Date: October 1871 Motion: Slow, then moved off at speed Description: Log like, then up-turned boat	Observer: John Macleod Time: Unknown Date: 1908 Motion: Motionless, then moved off Description: Long tapering tail, eel-like head. 30-40ft, creature lying in the water, flush with surface	Observer: Mrs B. McDonnell and Mrs Sutherland Time: 09.00 Date: August 25th 1933 Motion: Moving in an undulating way, submerged Description: Hump with disturbances 20ft behind
Observer: Mr and Mrs Donald MacIver and daughter and 2 cyclists Time: 17.00 Date: July 1947 Motion: Moved at speed Description: Single object	Observer: Mae Macdonald and Sylvia Paterson Time: 11.15 Date: May 31st 1966 Motion: Moving fast Description: 3 humps	Observer: Mr Jenkyns Time: 11.45 Date: November 10th 1973 Motion: Emerged, submerged Description: A rigid pole-like object
Observer: Staff at Craigdarroch House Hotel Time: 20.30 Date: June 13th 1996 Motion: Zigzagged across water Description: Large disturbance followed by wake	Observer: Adam and Mark Sutherland, Peter Gillies and Peter Rhind Time: 05.00 Date: June 17th 1998 Motion: Emerged, submerged Description: Large object with long tail	

Text B

Film evidence

The famous Tim Dinsdale filmed one of the most convincing sightings on 21st April 1960. He was driving down a road from Upper Foyers, leading to the Foyers Hotel, when he spotted an object in the Loch over one

5 kilometre away. He took out his binoculars to have a closer look and observed something long and oval, with strange colourings. It started to move, so Dinsdale decided to film the creature. Using a 16mm Bolex cine camera mounted on a tripod, he caught on film the

10 object zigzagging its way across the Loch. It then turned left about 300 metres from the opposite shoreline and travelled almost parallel to the shore. This all happened within the space of four minutes and the film in the camera was running out, so he drove his car down to the shore to try and get closer to the object. But when he reached the shore the object had disappeared. People's opinions began to

15 change and the credibility of the possible existence of the monster grew as the *Daily Mirror* printed a story on the film on 13th June 1960. The BBC also broadcast the film the very same day, using 35mm film which enhanced picture detail and contrast.

Dinsdale was convinced enough by his own pictures to give up his career as an aeronautical engineer and devoted the next twenty years of his life to trying to find the monster.

Text C

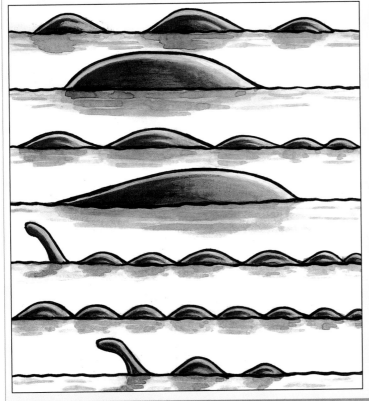

What Nessie looks like

This drawing shows various body shapes sketched by different observers. *Statistics:* In 20% of sightings a back or body is reported as distinct from the appearance of humps, and the most common description is that of 'an upturned boat', but others have said: 'It looked like an elephant's back – stood about 4ft high and 10–12ft in length – an egg-shaped body – seen end-on there is a distinct angle at apex of back – a long dark body – like a gigantic eel 25ft in length and 5ft in diameter.' Descriptions such as these are not very specific and the best that can be said for them is that the majority refer to some very large object.

Text D

The Loch Ness Monster's Song

Sssnnnwhufffll?

Hnwhuffl hhnnwfl hnfl hfl?

Gdroblboblhobngbl gbl gl g g g g glbgl.

Drublhaflablhaflubhafgabhaflhafl fl fl –

5   gm grawwwww grf grawf awfgm graw

Hovoplodok-doplodovok-plovodokot-

doplodokosh?

Splgraw fok fok splgrafhatchgabrlgabrl

splfok!

10 Zgra kra gka fok!

Grof grawff ghaf?

Gombl mbl bl –

blm plm,

blm plm,

15 blm plm,

blp.

Edwin Morgan

Text E

AN EYE WITNESS ACCOUNT

On 22nd July 1933 a most extraordinary thing happened, so extraordinary it taxed the imagination of even the most confirmed believers. Driving down the narrow road, early one morning, between the village of Dorres and Inverfarigaig, Mr Spicer and his wife saw 'a most extraordinary form of animal' crossing the road ahead; which at this point lay some 20 yards from the water. First a long neck appeared, undulating rapidly, forming a number of arches. It was a little thicker than an elephant's trunk and stretched the width of the road, and behind it a huge ponderous body lurched towards the Loch. In seconds it crossed the road, and disappeared through the bushes out of sight. The Spicers, at first some 200 yards distant, accelerated towards it, but when they arrived there was nothing to see, just a gap in the undergrowth through which the creature must have passed. Staggered and curiously repelled by what they had seen, the Spicers withstood the barrage of questions levelled at them after the event by various interested people.

Sharpen spelling

Syllabification

Each beat in a word is a **syllable**. Words with one beat are called monosyllabic, e.g. 'cat'. Words with more than one beat are called polysyllabic, e.g. 'cat/a/logue'.

It is our recognition of certain syllables that helps us to read Edwin Morgan's poem. We can pronounce the word 'do/plo/do/kosh', even if we don't understand it.

But we have to think more carefully about how to pronounce other words in the poem because the letter combinations of part or all of the word are not familiar, for example 'Hnwhuffl hhnnwfl hnfl hfl'.

Study the poem closely. Pick out and list the syllables which are familiar to you.

Try reading the poem aloud with a partner. Agree how best to pronounce the syllables which are not familiar to you.

Breaking words into syllables and saying them out loud is a good way to help you spell tricky words, e.g. 'e/val/u/a/tion', 'spe/ci/fi/ca/tion'.

Text F

New Nessie pictures spark debate

Stephen Fraser

Nessie mania returned to Scotland yesterday after new pictures were printed of Scotland's most reclusive resident.

The new photos appeared to show a slimmer Loch Ness monster, prompting fervent speculation that the living dinosaur could have been pregnant.

Instead of the usual fleeting glimpse afforded her followers, Nessie stayed above the surface long enough for retired printer Roy Johnston to take at least four photographs showing the suspiciously snake-like Nessie arching out of the water and returning to it with a splash. The new photographs, printed in yesterday's *Daily Mail*, prompted an immediate debate as to whether they are genuine.

Johnston, 63, said he and his wife, Janet, had been nearing the end of a Highlands holiday two weeks ago when he decided to stop in a lay-by near the loch.

He made his way to the loch's edge at around 9 a.m. and had been standing there only a few minutes before the 'creature' emerged.

'I thought I was going mad,' he said. 'The first thought that sprang into my mind was, 'That's an elephant.' I know it sounds silly but it looked like a trunk. It was the same length and width.

The sighting has delighted tourism businesses in the area. Malaina Krott-Thiarry, a worker at a tourist information centre close to the loch, said: 'I have no idea what to make of these pictures, but I think they're good news for the area.'

Lawrence Sear, the managing director of the *Daily Mail*, said there was absolutely no sign the photographs had been doctored. But *Scotland on Sunday's* picture editor, Kayt Turner, said there was room for doubt. A picture editor for 15 years, she added: 'Anyone with a spare £500 can get the equipment needed to digitally manipulate this kind of image, using a simple software package such as Photoshop. All you need is a scanner and a computer.'

Text G

"I don't care what you thought you saw, there are no such things as people."

From The New Scotsman

Text H

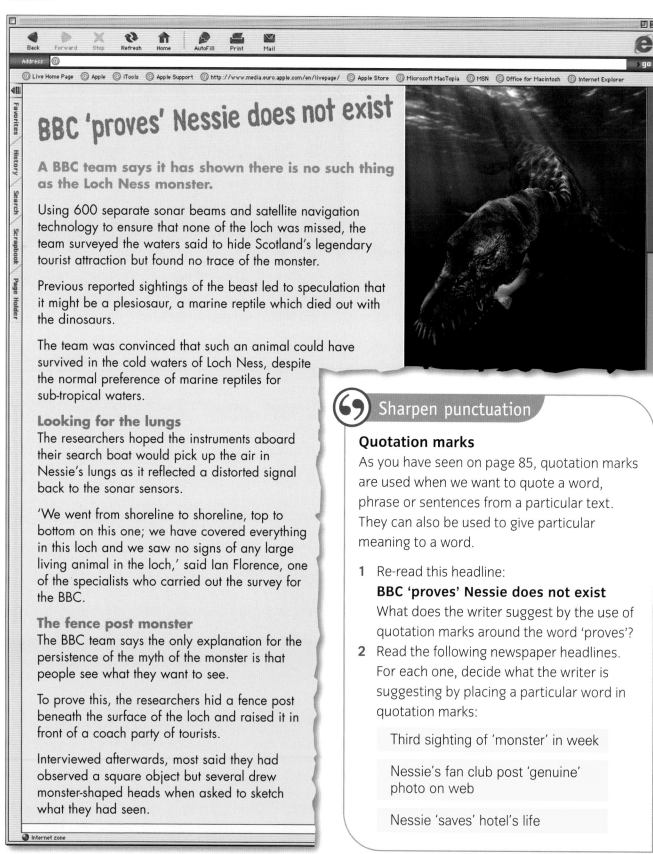

BBC 'proves' Nessie does not exist

A BBC team says it has shown there is no such thing as the Loch Ness monster.

Using 600 separate sonar beams and satellite navigation technology to ensure that none of the loch was missed, the team surveyed the waters said to hide Scotland's legendary tourist attraction but found no trace of the monster.

Previous reported sightings of the beast led to speculation that it might be a plesiosaur, a marine reptile which died out with the dinosaurs.

The team was convinced that such an animal could have survived in the cold waters of Loch Ness, despite the normal preference of marine reptiles for sub-tropical waters.

Looking for the lungs

The researchers hoped the instruments aboard their search boat would pick up the air in Nessie's lungs as it reflected a distorted signal back to the sonar sensors.

'We went from shoreline to shoreline, top to bottom on this one; we have covered everything in this loch and we saw no signs of any large living animal in the loch,' said Ian Florence, one of the specialists who carried out the survey for the BBC.

The fence post monster

The BBC team says the only explanation for the persistence of the myth of the monster is that people see what they want to see.

To prove this, the researchers hid a fence post beneath the surface of the loch and raised it in front of a coach party of tourists.

Interviewed afterwards, most said they had observed a square object but several drew monster-shaped heads when asked to sketch what they had seen.

66 Sharpen punctuation

Quotation marks

As you have seen on page 85, quotation marks are used when we want to quote a word, phrase or sentences from a particular text. They can also be used to give particular meaning to a word.

1 Re-read this headline:
   BBC 'proves' Nessie does not exist
   What does the writer suggest by the use of quotation marks around the word 'proves'?

2 Read the following newspaper headlines. For each one, decide what the writer is suggesting by placing a particular word in quotation marks:

   Third sighting of 'monster' in week

   Nessie's fan club post 'genuine' photo on web

   Nessie 'saves' hotel's life

Feedback

Work in groups of three or four. You are going to assess the preparation you did in Stages 1–4 of Activity 9 on pages 121–2.

Stage 1 Look at the table you completed on page 121. Did you agree on which texts were the most and least useful? If not, discuss the texts and amend your table if you change your mind.

Stage 2 Think about the different questions you asked about **Texts B** and **E**. With these in mind, write two questions about **Text F** and two questions about **Text H**. These questions should help you to decide how useful and reliable **Texts F** and **H** are.

Stage 3 Compare the notes you have made. Whose notes do you think are the most useful? Explain why you think they are the most useful. Then improve your own notes using theirs as a model.

Stage 4 Compare the two lists of evidence you made about Nessie. If you have left out important details from either of the lists, add them now.

Look back over your preparation. How helpful was it in preparing you to answer the question 'Does Nessie exist?' Write down two things you could have done to improve it.

Does Nessie exist? How to write a balanced response

Now that you have read the texts closely, and weighed up the evidence, the next step is to organise your ideas for an answer to the question 'Does Nessie exist?' Here is a simple structure that works well when writing a balanced response:

Introduction
Explain the issue. Give some background information on:
- who or what 'Nessie' is
- where she is supposed to live
- why it is not certain that she exists.

Paragraph 1
State clearly the evidence that suggests Nessie exists. Refer to some of the texts you have studied, and anything else you know on the subject.

Paragraph 2
State clearly the evidence that suggests that Nessie does *not* exist. Refer to some of the texts you have studied, and anything else you know about the subject.

Conclusion
Deal directly with the question: 'Does Nessie exist?' You can give your own opinions but remember to support them with evidence. You don't have to give a definite 'yes' or 'no' answer.

Activity 10

Here is an example of the first two paragraphs of a response to the question 'Does Nessie exist?' Some of the features of writing a balanced response are highlighted for you.

1 Study the writing and the annotations closely.

Loch Ness is[1] a large and deep lake in Scotland. Since 1871, there have been recorded sightings of a large, unusual creature, sometimes called Nessie.[2] Some[3] people, like Tim Dinsdale, have spent many years of their lives trying to prove that Nessie exists. Others claim this is just an attempt to attract tourists and that there is no monster in the lake. Let's[4] examine the evidence.

Over the years there have been many sightings of Nessie, and not just by people on their own.[5] In July 1947[6] Mr and Mrs Donald MacIver and their daughter and two cyclists reported seeing a single object 'move at speed' across the lake. As recently as[6] 1998, Adam and Mark Sutherland, Peter Gillies and Peter Rhind reported seeing a large object with a long tail. It seems unlikely that so many different people would mistake a boat or a log for a monster.[7] Furthermore, there is film evidence of Nessie. In 1960, Tim Dinsdale filmed 'one of the most convincing sightings' on his 16mm Bolex cine camera.[8] Added to this[9] are the recent photographs taken by retired printer Roy Johnston, which show a 'snake-like Nessie arching out of the water and returning to it with a splash'.[10]

1 Simple present tense used.

2 Background information given.

3 Two different points of view stated.

4 Reader directly involved.

5 General statement.

6 Specific examples support general statement.

7 Conclusion based on evidence.

8 Further evidence.

9 Connectives link points.

10 Quotations used to support points.

2 Now read the third paragraph of the same response. The sentences are numbered 1 to 6. Match the four annotations A to D to the correct four sentences:

   A opposite point of view stated
   B additional evidence used to make point
   C quotation used to support point
   D new evidence introduced.

[1]Many would, however, question the reliability of some of these 'sightings'. [2]They would argue, for example, that the staff at the Craigdarroch House Hotel had much to gain by seeing Nessie, particularly if business was slow. [3]Research also suggests that people see what they want to see rather than what is actually in front of them. [4]Furthermore, photographs and video recordings can be faked. [5]As Scotland on Sunday's picture editor, Kayt Turner, said: 'Anyone with a spare £500 can get the equipment needed to digitally manipulate this kind of image'. [6]Added to this is the evidence from the BBC team, which used 600 sonar beams and satellite navigation technology and still found no sign of Nessie.

Connectives

A connective is a word or phrase that links clauses or sentences. It is helpful to build up a range of connectives to use when writing a balanced response. The connectives below were used in the three paragraphs on page 128. Can you find them?

Since	Over the years	As recently as	It seems … that	Also
Added to this	However	For example	Furthermore	

Activity 11

Now you are going to write the conclusion to the essay on page 128. In your conclusion, remember:

- to write in the present tense and use standard English
- to use connectives to link sentences
- to deal directly with the question: 'Does Nessie exist?'
- that you don't have to give a 'yes' or 'no' answer to the question
- to give your own opinions and support them with evidence.

It is always good to end your conclusion in a way that will make your reader think, for example:

Does Nessie exist? This is a question that many people have asked but no one has managed to answer … yet.

Try to think of an even better way to end your conclusion.

Now write your conclusion. Leave a wide margin on either side of your writing. Aim to write 50–100 words.

When you have finished writing, annotate your use of:

- the present tense
- connectives
- your opinions
- evidence and quotation.

 Progress check

So far in this unit you have:

- identified the attitude of the writer
- referred to a text to support the points you make
- selected and made notes on particular texts
- asked appropriate questions about a text
- examined a balanced response to a question
- written a conclusion.

1 Look back through the unit and the work you have done. Write out each of the bullet points above, and tick once, twice or three times, depending on how confident you feel.

2 Choose the one you feel most confident about (three ticks) and the one you feel least confident about (one tick). For each one, explain why you feel as you do.

Assessment task

The deep blue sea

In this assessment task you are going to read five texts about the sea and the creatures that live in it. You are going to consider all the information and answer the following question:

How much damage are people doing to the sea and the creatures that live in it?

You will be assessed on the ways you:

- select the most useful texts
- make notes on appropriate details
- use evidence in your writing to support the points you make
- present a balanced response.

1 Read the information on pages 131–2.

2 To help you weigh up this information and answer the question, follow steps 1–7 below.

Step 1

Decide which texts, or parts of texts, are the most useful and why.

Step 2

Make notes on the details you could include in your writing.

Step 3

Make a list of useful questions to ask about the texts.

Step 4

Ensure you have a balance of points of view.

Step 5

Plan the contents of:

- your introduction
- paragraph 1
- paragraph 2
- your conclusion.

Step 6

Write your response. Remember to include evidence and quotations from the texts to support the points you make.

Step 7

When you have finished, check that you have:

- presented a balanced view
- given a range of evidence to support the points you make
- based your conclusion on the evidence.

Text A

Oil Pollution

Black tar-like oil is sometimes washed onto beaches, not only causing a nuisance to holiday makers but also killing many sea-birds. The oil mainly comes from tankers which empty out their holds while out at sea to save time in port. Once oil is in the sea and the tanker has sailed on, it is difficult to prove that an offence has been committed and unless the culprit can be identified the cost of clearing up is the responsibility of the local council.

In recent years, there have been a number of serious oil spillages caused by oil tanker accidents. The first was in 1967, when the *Torrey Canyon* ran aground on the Seven Stone Rocks, off Land's End, leaking 106,000 tonnes of oil onto rocks and beaches on both sides of the English Channel. As a result the population of puffins on the Sept Isles in France was virtually wiped out.

Text B

Did you know??

Dirty Fishing Kills

65,000–80,000 whales, dolphins, seals and other marine mammals perish through dirty fishing methods each year. For example, shrimp trawl-fishing uses heavy nets to catch and throw back dead an estimated 5.2 pounds of marine life for every pound of shrimp landed.

Cruise and Lose

A typical cruise ship can produce up to 30,000 gallons of sewage daily. Cruise ships can legally dump raw sewage in the ocean only 3 miles from shore. Yet, for the cost of a can of cola per passenger per day, cruise ships can stop polluting the oceans.

Pollution spreads

Ocean currents spread pollution. Although coastlines tend to be more polluted, no ocean water is pure. Scientists have found pollution in all oceans of the world, no matter how remote or clean they seem. Toxic chemicals have been found in albatrosses on remote Midway Island in the middle of the Pacific.

Text C

New Zealanders save some whales in mass stranding

Wednesday, January 8, 2003
by Ray Lilley, Associated Press

WELLINGTON, New Zealand – Rescuers refloated 39 pilot whales on Wednesday's high tide, but dozens more died after a pod beached on a remote island off southern New Zealand, officials said.

Residents and conservation specialists frantically dragged, pushed and steered the surviving mammals from the 159-whale pod off the sand and into deep water.

By nightfall, the 39 whales had moved about 2.4 kilometres (1.5 miles) into open sea. They were heading south away from the stranding site at Paterson's Inlet near Oban, the only town on Stewart Island, 40 kilometres (25 miles) off the south coast of South Island.

'That was a very good result,' said Greg Lind, the Department of Conservation southern islands' area manager. 'The 39 we got off were the only ones alive when the stranded pod was found around midday,' he added. 'Overseas, such refloat efforts are rarely successful.'

Some 80 people, mostly volunteers, worked through the hot afternoon, pouring sea water on the beached mammals as they waited for the tide to turn so the refloat attempt could be launched. Once back in the water the whales were herded by small boats away from the beach and into open water.

Volunteer helper Michaela Ballard, of Christchurch, New Zealand, said the rescue effort at times felt like a lost cause. 'You try and help them all you can. At least there's a chance rather than leaving them to die,' she said.

Text D

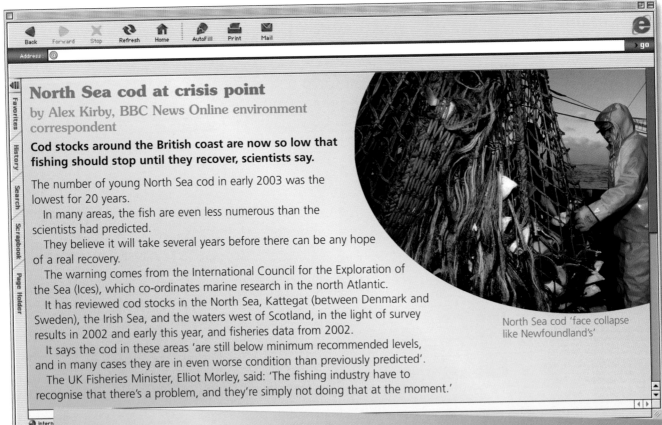

North Sea cod at crisis point

by Alex Kirby, BBC News Online environment correspondent

Cod stocks around the British coast are now so low that fishing should stop until they recover, scientists say.

The number of young North Sea cod in early 2003 was the lowest for 20 years.

In many areas, the fish are even less numerous than the scientists had predicted.

They believe it will take several years before there can be any hope of a real recovery.

The warning comes from the International Council for the Exploration of the Sea (Ices), which co-ordinates marine research in the north Atlantic.

It has reviewed cod stocks in the North Sea, Kattegat (between Denmark and Sweden), the Irish Sea, and the waters west of Scotland, in the light of survey results in 2002 and early this year, and fisheries data from 2002.

It says the cod in these areas 'are still below minimum recommended levels, and in many cases they are in even worse condition than previously predicted'.

The UK Fisheries Minister, Elliot Morley, said: 'The fishing industry have to recognise that there's a problem, and they're simply not doing that at the moment.'

North Sea cod 'face collapse like Newfoundland's'

Text E

Volunteer Projects with MCS

Beachwatch
This nationwide annual beach clean and survey takes place every September. By organising Beachwatch in your area, you can help highlight the problems of coastal pollution whilst gathering data on the amount, types and sources of marine and beach litter. A report of the results is published, which is used as a focus for the MCS Campaign For Clean Seas to increase individual, industry and government responsibility to keep litter out of our seas.

Adopt-A-Beach
The Adopt-A-Beach project has developed from Beachwatch as a local environmental initiative. Volunteers clean and survey their stretch of coastline and report their findings to the Marine Conservation Society. You can do other surveys and projects, and really make a difference to 'your' stretch of beach.

Basking Shark Watch
Basking sharks are the second largest fish in the world, and yet we know very little about them. MCS launched the Basking Shark Watch Project in 1987 to gather information about the sharks that visit UK waters every summer. The information gathered has provided evidence that conservation measures are needed to ensure the future of the basking shark population and strengthened the case for protection of the species in UK waters. Basking Shark Watch

Ocean Vigil
Be our eyes and ears on the sea. Ocean Vigil is a sightings project for the North East Atlantic for all seafarers. Anyone who sails, dives, spends time at sea or walks along the coast can report their sightings of marine wildlife, pollution and fishing activities. Contact MCS for more details.

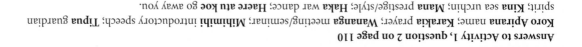

Answers to Activity 1, question 2 on page 110
Koro Apirana name; **Karakia** prayer; **Mihimihi** introductory speech; **Tipua** guardian spirit; **Kina** sea urchin; **Mana** prestige/style; **Haka** war dance; **Haere atu koe** go away you.

6 Scripts and sketches

The bigger picture

In this unit you will read extracts from four different plays and one complete play. You will investigate how the writers develop their ideas in script through the characters' words and actions. At the end of the unit you will write a script and present a dramatic performance.

WHAT? You will:
- explore how a writer creates and develops character through speech and action
- trace the development of ideas in scripts
- evaluate the effectiveness of dramatic performance

HOW? by:
- investigating a range of writing techniques
- asking questions about scripts and identifying links with other forms of literature
- working with others to present a dramatic performance

WHY? because:
- studying the work of other writers helps you develop your writing
- asking questions and revising your answers develops your thinking skills
- the ability to work co-operatively and productively with others enables you to achieve more.

What does *drama* mean to you?

Talk about the pictures and the words in the collage. What do you think they might have to do with *drama*?

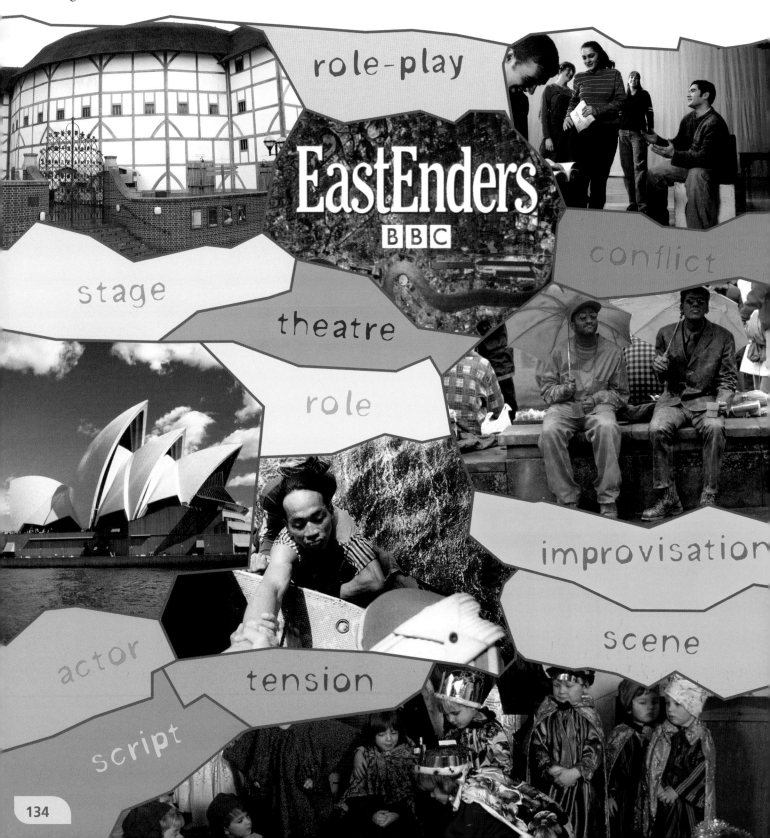

role-play

EastEnders
BBC

conflict

stage

theatre

role

improvisation

scene

actor

tension

script

Plays

A play is one type of drama. Many different people are involved in a play:

- the playwright, who writes the play
- the actors, who are playing parts in the play
- the director, who is responsible for the overall interpretation of the play, the preparation of the actors, and the general design
- the audience, who will watch the play being performed.

Playwrights may have many different reasons for writing plays. They might want to:

- make the audience think about a particular issue
- make the audience laugh or cry
- show something ordinary in an extraordinary way.

Script

Plays are written as scripts – a form of writing that is very different from prose. Activity 1 explores the differences between script and prose.

Activity 1

Look at the following texts. They are both about the same thing. The first text is written as a script and the second text is written in prose.

Script

Jim and Dave outside in playground in large secondary school.

	DAVE	Do you know where we gotta go for our next class?
5	**JIM**	Search me. This place is massive, innit? Makes our old school look mini.
	DAVE	What d'you reckon to this place, then?
	JIM	I like it so far, I think. What about you?

From *The Bully* by Gene Kemp

Prose

Jim and Dave stood in the playground of a large secondary school. They were dressed in brand-new school uniform and were clearly straight from primary school. Dave,
5 the taller of the two boys, spoke first. 'Do you know where we gotta go for our next class?' he asked, looking in a confused manner at the map he clutched in his hand.

'Search me,' Jim replied, gazing around
10 him. 'This place is massive, innit? Makes our old school look mini.'

Both boys shuffled uncomfortably.

'What d'you reckon to this place, then?' Dave asked.

15 Jim's reply was hesitant. 'I like it so far, I think'. He looked around at the vast playground that stretched into the distance. 'What about you?'

1 Talk about and write down the information you are given in the prose text
that you are not given in the script, for example:
- dressed in brand-new uniform
- clearly straight from primary school.

2 Decide and make notes on how this information could be given to the
audience when the script is performed. You could present this in a table,
for example:

Information in prose text not given in script	How this information could be given to the audience
dressed in brand-new uniform	the actors would wear brand-new uniform
clearly straight from primary school	

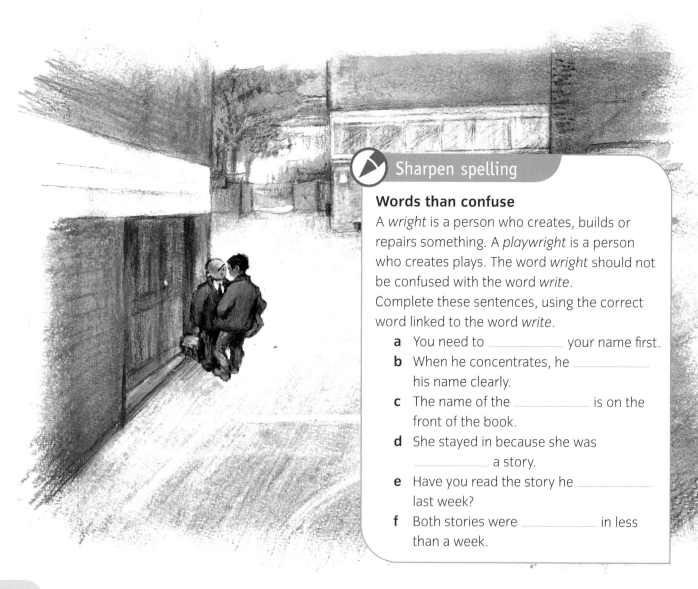

Sharpen spelling

Words than confuse

A *wright* is a person who creates, builds or
repairs something. A *playwright* is a person
who creates plays. The word *wright* should not
be confused with the word *write*.

Complete these sentences, using the correct
word linked to the word *write*.

  a You need to _____ your name first.

  b When he concentrates, he _____
     his name clearly.

  c The name of the _____ is on the
     front of the book.

  d She stayed in because she was
     _____ a story.

  e Have you read the story he _____
     last week?

  f Both stories were _____ in less
     than a week.

Presenting speech in writing

There are three ways of presenting speech in writing:

- In **direct speech** we use the speaker's exact words and mark the beginning and end of them with speech marks, for example:

  'What d'you reckon to this place, then?'
  Dave asked.

- In **reported speech**, we report what was said but do not use the exact words of the speaker. We usually change pronouns and verb tenses, and speech marks are not used, for example:

  Dave asked him what he reckoned to the place.

- In **script** we use the speaker's exact words only. We write the name of the speaker in the margin (in bold if printed) and the words next to the name. We do not use speech marks. For example:

  DAVE   What d'you reckon to this place, then?

Activity 2

1 Rewrite the following examples of reported speech in both direct speech *and* script:
   a John said that he needed to take cakes to school for a cake stall the next day.
   b Katy asked her mother for some money to buy cakes at the cake stall.
   c Mrs Foster told the children they had made £42 at the cake stall.

2 Check your answers with a partner and with the examples of direct speech and script given above. If you have made a mistake, correct it.

Dialogue

Dialogue is the name given to the words the actors speak. The same words can be spoken in many different ways.

Activity 3

1 Say the following sentence four times. Each time, emphasise the word in bold. Talk about the different meaning each emphasis gives to the sentence.
   a **I** will not go into that room.
   b I **will** not go into that room.
   c I will **not** go into that room.
   d I will not go into **that** room.

2 Try saying the following sentence in the way suggested in the brackets.

   a You want me to speak to the group?
     (*sulky and sarcastic, with no intention of doing it*)

   b You want me to speak to the group?
     (*delighted and surprised to be asked to do this*)

3 With a partner, talk about which word, or words, you need to emphasise to create the right effect.

4 With a partner, experiment with the following sentences. How many different meanings can you give each one by the way you say it?
   a Is there anybody there?
   b This is an interesting piece of work.
   c I've never seen anything like that before.

Capturing how people speak

A playwright chooses words carefully to capture the way people speak and the sounds they make.

Activity 4

1 Read the extract from *The Mobile* on the following page and find examples of the use of:
- slang
- contractions
- words that make sounds.

2 What can you work out about the kind of character Gaz is from what he says and the way he says it? Give reasons for your answer.

3 What do you discover about Baz from the way he speaks to Gaz and Daz?

4 Write six more lines of dialogue between Baz and Gaz, in which the characters continue their search. Do not use stage directions. Aim to capture each character in the words you choose for them. Keep the lines you write as you will be working on them again later.

> **Feedback**
>
> **1** Cover up the names of the characters in the lines you have written. Ask a partner to read what you have written and guess which lines belong to which character.
>
> **2** Ask your partner to tell you:
> - which clues helped most
> - how you could make it clearer which character is Baz and which is Gaz.
>
> **3** Think about and make notes on how you could improve your lines. Keep these notes as you will need them for Activity 5.

The Mobile

A classroom at break-time. The room is empty. The door slowly opens and Baz's head peers in, looking around. His head is quite low down. Another head, Daz's, appears above the first. A third head, Gaz's appears above the other two. Convinced that the room is empty, Baz starts to straighten up.

5   **BAZ**   Come on, there's no one . . .

Before he can finish, he bumps into the others, who are looking over the top of him. They all stumble into the room noisily and end up in a heap on the floor.

(to Daz) Ssshhhhhh!

10 **DAZ**   *(to Gaz)* Ssshhhhhh!

  GAZ   *(looking around, then to no one in particular)* Ssshhhhhh!

  BAZ   *(whispering)* Will you pair belt up! If we get caught in 'ere we're in big trouble.

  DAZ   *(to Gaz)* Yeah, belt up, will you!

15 *The three boys get to their feet and quietly close the door behind them.*

  GAZ   What we doin' in 'ere, Baz?

  BAZ   Lookin' for a phone, you twonk! Now shut up.

Baz and Daz begin searching the room. Gaz scratches his head and looks puzzled.

20 **GAZ**   There's a phone at the end of Clayton Street, Baz. It's bust too, you don't have to put any money in.

  DAZ   *(slowly shaking his head)* Not that sort of phone. A mobile phone.

  GAZ   I got one 'ere.

Gaz begins to reach inside his jacket.

25 **BAZ**   No, you sad geek. We're looking for a mobile phone to nick.

  GAZ   Oh. Right.

They continue searching. Gaz still looks confused.

From *The Mobile* by Mark Morris .

Stage directions

When speaking the words in a play, actors will:
- pause in certain places for effect
- use a particular tone of voice or speak loudly or softly
- make facial expressions to reflect what they are saying or thinking
- move their bodies to reflect what they are saying or thinking.

Playwrights frequently use stage directions to give the director and actor ideas to work with. In the extract from *The Mobile* on page 139, the stage directions are printed in italics.

Activity 5

Read the stage directions in the extract from *The Mobile* carefully.

1 Draw a table like the one below and decide which column each of the stage directions fits in.

Describes the scene	Describes how the words should be spoken	Describes the actions the actors should make
A classroom at breaktime.		The door opens slowly and Baz's head peers in.

2 Look back at the six lines of script you wrote in Activity 4 on page 138. What stage directions could you include to help the actors and the director? Redraft your six lines of script. Aim to:
- make improvements to the script based on the notes you made in the Feedback
- include stage directions that describe the scene, how the words should be spoken and the actions the actors should make.

3 Sometimes playwrights deliberately do not use stage directions. In pairs, talk about the possible advantages of this and make a list of three possible advantages of not having stage directions.

4 Share your list with another pair of students. Number the possible advantages in order of importance and underline or highlight the one you consider to be most important.

Different ways of writing scripts

Playwrights can write scripts in many different ways, using a range of techniques. You are going to examine two scriptwriting techniques by looking at extracts from two plays: *Joyride* on page 142 and *The Off-side Trap* on page 143.

Activity 6

Joyride is made up of twelve very short scenes, all of them about the same accident. The technique used by the writers is to set each scene in a different place and let the audience make the connections between them. This could be made to work on stage by using spotlights or, more simply, by the players 'freezing' and only coming to life when they speak.

The extract from *Joyride* consists of the first three scenes of the play. Each scene involves two people.

1 Read each scene closely. Think about:
- how the words should be said
- the facial expressions and body movements the actors need to make.

You could try acting the scenes once you have thought about them.

2 Music and sound effects are often used to create a dramatic effect. Think about and make notes on the type of music or sound effects you would use in these scenes. Give reasons for your choices.

3 Now write the next short scene (no more than 5 lines) between a reporter and an eyewitness to the accident.

 **Highlight thinking**

Critical thinking: group discussion
This way of thinking allows you to consider two sides of an argument, or to explore one side of an issue in more detail.

Sharing and improving your ideas through discussion can help the group to come up with more ideas than one person on their own could. It will also give each of you practice in explaining and justifying your ideas to others – a key skill.

Scene 1

POLICE OFFICER We'll have to ask you to make an identification.
The woman weeps and shakes her head to show that she can't.
I'm sorry, we have to have a formal identification. It'll only take a moment.

Scene 2

FIRST YOUTH *(panting)* Cor, thought the Plod had us that time.
SECOND YOUTH Yeah-hey, see Phil in the yellow Merc?
Pheeeoooow! *(Mimes how fast Phil was travelling.)*
FIRST YOUTH Goin' like the clappers with that cop car right behind him.
5 SECOND YOUTH Awesome! *(sobering)* Reckon he got away?
FIRST YOUTH Yeah – course. He'll be OK.

Scene 3

DETECTIVE Well, you've done it properly this time, haven't you, sunshine?
PHIL *(after a long pause)* Is she …?
DETECTIVE You were doing seventy and hit her smack on. What do you think?

From *Joyride* by Steve Barlow and Steve Skidmore

Feedback

1 With a partner, present your scene to another pair or small group.
Each student will be assessed on the effectiveness of:
- tone of voice
- facial expressions and body movements
- (optional) choice of music and/or sound effects.
The group should assess your performance and copy and complete the following sentences for each student:

- The tone of voice you used when you …   was effective because …
                                              could have been more effective if …

- The facial expressions and body movements   were effective because …
  you used when you …   could have been more effective if …

- The music/sound effect you used to show …   was effective because …
                                              could have been more effective if …

2 Keep a record of the feedback you get to help you improve your next performance.

Activity 7

In *The Off-side Trap*, the writer uses a clever technique to reveal the characters' thoughts to the audience: for the two main characters, Maxine and Paul, she uses additional characters, Maxine 1 and Paul 1, to speak their thoughts.

1 Using four actors, read the following scene, which is taken from the start of the play.

2 How could the thoughts spoken by Maxine 1 and Paul 1 be got across to the audience through body movements and facial expressions? Write down the stage directions you would give to the actors in a table, like this:

Sharpen punctuation

Commas

Commas can change the meaning of a sentence.

1 What is the difference in meaning between the following sentences?
   a Oh, you know nothing much.
   b Oh, you know, nothing much.
2 Where could you place commas in the following sentences to change their meaning?
   a Maxine said Paul had made a mistake.
   b We'll find out if the director knows his job.
3 Write one sentence of your own, in which the commas change the meaning.

Words	Facial expressions and body movements
Maxine 1: OK, done it. Made contact.	
Maxine 1: He doesn't sound very pleased to see me.	

	MAXINE	Hi Paul.
	MAXINE 1	OK, done it. Made contact.
	PAUL	All right, Maxine.
	MAXINE 1	He doesn't sound very pleased to see me.
5	**PAUL**	What you up to?
	PAUL 1	Tell me I didn't say that – talk about stating the blinking obvious!
	MAXINE	Oh, you know, nothing much.
	PAUL	Right.
10		*Pause.*
	MAXINE 1	Come on, come on. Say something.
	PAUL 1	What do I say now?
		Pause.
	PAUL	So … um …
15	**MAXINE**	(*at the same time*) What did you … Oh, sorry.
	MAXINE 1	Oh no – how clumsy was that?
	PAUL	No, you first.
	PAUL 1	Come on, man, be cool.

From *The Off-side* Trap by Mary Colson

✓ Progress check

So far in this unit you have examined different techniques and explored:
- the different ways words can be spoken
- how character is revealed through words and actions
- the purpose of stage directions in a playscript.

Now you are going to use what you have learnt.

1 Working in groups of four, you will take part in a group presentation of a short scripted scene from a play about bullying at school. The characters in the scene are boys. If you are working in a mixed or all-girl group, change the names to suit.
You will be assessed on:
a How well the words are given meaning by the characters.
b How well the actions reinforce the meaning of the words.

2 Read the scene opposite carefully a few times. In your groups, decide:
- who should play each part and why
- the most important things about this scene
- how you are going to get these across to your audience through tone of voice, facial expressions and body movements
- the stage directions you want to add (space has been left in the script to show where you could add your own stage directions).

3 Present your performance to another group or to the class.

> - Aim to learn your lines as this helps the performance flow more easily.
> - When you are performing, it is important that you stay in role until the performance is finished, whether you are speaking or not.

4 When you have seen a performance, assess it. Copy and shade in two grids like the ones below. The better the performance, the more you shade in.

| The | words | are | given | meaning | by | the | characters. |

| The | actions | reinforce | the | meaning | of | the | words. |

The Bully

Jim and Dave are first-year students. They have been at their new school for a week.

Walking up the hill to school with Dave. Some older pupils waiting outside, sitting on the wall. One of them, wearing school uniform,

5 *but with DMs and trousers too short for him and a skinhead haircut, approaches Jim.*

HOUSEMAN	What's your name?	
	_____	
DAVE	Leave him alone.	
10	_____	
JIM	Why do you want to know?	
HOUSEMAN	Cos I do. You better tell me.	
OTHER BOY	Don't let him give you any cheek, Houseman.	
JIM	Jim Sutton.	
15 **HOUSEMAN**	Well, Jim Sutton, have you got any money for me?	
JIM	No, I spent it on bus fare.	
HOUSEMAN	I hope you ain't lying to me.	
	_____	
	What's this then?	
20	_____	
	Be seeing you around, Jim Sutton.	
	_____	

> You could suggest stage directions to replace the blank lines.

From *The Bully* by Gene Kemp

Studying a complete play

So far in this unit you have studied extracts from plays. Now you are going to consider a whole play. You will think about:

- the meanings of the play
- the way the playwright has presented his ideas
- how these ideas are developed within the play
- ways in which the play could be presented on stage.

Activity 8

1 Read the script on pages 146–53 aloud, playing the parts. You could work in groups or share the reading in the class. As you read, talk about the questions in the margin and make notes for your answers.

Bright Lights

List of characters

Storyteller	Gary
Helen	Nick

The main thoroughfare of the busy, bustling city. Night. A place of restaurants, multiplex cinemas, clubs, theatres, traffic, and so on.

Storyteller is there, standing in the doorway of a nightclub, as a bouncer. Speaks to the audience.

5　　*He turns and looks down the street a little way, to where Helen and Gary are walking. Our attention switches to them.*

STORYTELLER　The city at night. Bright lights, music, hurry and hustle, bustle and rush. You can feel the excitement tingling in the air, the thrill of it shivering under your skin, the rhythm thumping up through the

10　　soles of your feet. All the promise of a good night out, if you know what you're looking for, and if you've got the money to pay for it. But if you haven't, and if you don't – if you're new to the city and don't know your way – well, it's a dangerous place, and you can end up lost for ever.

15　**HELEN**　What shall we do, then?

GARY　I don't know. Anything.

HELEN　How much have you got?

GARY　Thirty pounds.

HELEN　We could go and see a film.

20　**GARY**　See a film?

HELEN　Yes –

GARY　We can do better than that.

HELEN　Like what?

GARY　I don't know. Look around you. It's all here. Anything!

25　　*Attention switches back to Storyteller.*

STORYTELLER　Helen and Gary, sister and brother, out in the late-night city for the first time in their little lives. The products of a broken home. And who isn't these days? They live with their mother, and Friday nights they go and stay with their father. Only this Friday night,

30　　they haven't.

　　Attention switches to Gary and Helen.

HELEN　We should've gone to Dad's.

GARY　What for? So we can stay in and watch telly while he gets drunk down the pub?

35　**HELEN**　He'll wonder where we are.

> **1** The storyteller describes the scene. What kind of place is it? How could you represent this place on a stage? What music and sound effects would you use?

GARY		No, he won't. He don't know what day of the week it is half the time.
HELEN		All the same –
GARY		Look, we'll go there. But later. After we've had some fun.
40		*Attention switches to Storyteller.*
STORYTELLER		It's fun they're after. Fun and games and thrills and spills. But they won't find it here.
		Gary and Helen are standing outside Storyteller's club. He turns to them.
45		Want something?
GARY		How much does it cost to go in?
STORYTELLER		In here?
GARY		Yes.
STORYTELLER		More than you can afford.
50 **GARY**		How much?
STORYTELLER		Beat it.
GARY		Look, just tell us –
STORYTELLER		I'll tell you this. You're crowding the pavement. Causing an obstruction. And if you don't remove yourself, I'll have you
55		removed. Understand?
GARY		You can't make us move –
STORYTELLER		You want a bet?
HELEN		Gary –
GARY		We've got money –
60 **STORYTELLER**		Push off!
HELEN		Come on, Gary. He means it. Come on! *(She pulls Gary away.)*
STORYTELLER		Go home and go to bed. This ain't no place for you.
		Gary and Helen go. Storyteller speaks to us.
		I'm only trying to do them a favour. Places like this can be
65		dangerous for young innocents like them. And there's worse places than this. Places where real beasts lurk and live, if you know what I mean. Turn off the main way, and you'll find them, down in the dark alleys and side streets, creatures that live in the shadows, things that live on human flesh. If you know what's good
70		for you, you'll keep away from them. Cos behind the bright lights there's darkness and … horror.
		And some people just don't know what's good for them.

2 How do you think the storyteller should say lines 41–2? Explain your reason(s).

3 What new role does the Storyteller take on between lines 45–55?

4 What kinds of things and people do you think the Storyteller is talking about in lines 64–72?

Attention switches to Gary and Helen. They have moved down the street a little way and are standing outside a Chinese restaurant.

75	**HELEN**	How about something to eat? I'm starving.
	GARY	In there, you mean?
	HELEN	I love Chinese food.
	GARY	We can find a take-away.
	HELEN	It's not the same. I've never ate in a restaurant before. Becky from
80		school went to one for her birthday and she said –
	GARY	Have you seen these prices?
	HELEN	We can afford it. Just about.
	GARY	And have nothing left.
	HELEN	You got any better ideas?
85	**GARY**	Maybe.

Helen looks at the menu. As she does, Gary moves away.

HELEN We could have that … and that … or that … Oh, come on, Gary, please –

She turns. Gary has walked off. She runs after him.

90   Gary … Where are you going …?

Switch to Storyteller.

STORYTELLER Off the main way, down the dark street, straight into the devil's den.

Switch to Gary and Helen. They have turned off the main thoroughfare and are walking down a dark side street.

95		
	HELEN	What are we doing down here?
	GARY	Looking.
	HELEN	Looking for what?
	GARY	Fun.
100	**HELEN**	Down here? There's nothing down here.
	GARY	Yes, there is.
	HELEN	I don't like it. It's dark. It doesn't feel … safe …
	GARY	Scared, are you?
	HELEN	Yes! I am!
105	**GARY**	What of?
	HELEN	I don't know. You read things.
	GARY	Go on, then. Go back. Go to Dad's. Here's five pounds. That'll get you there.

    (He offers her the money. She just looks at it.) Ten, then.
110   *(He takes out another five pounds, shoves the two notes into her hand.)*
    Go on, if you're going! Clear off!

5 Try to picture Gary and Helen. What do you think they look like? How old do you think they are? What might they be wearing?

6 What have you learnt so far about the relationship between Helen and Gary?

	HELEN	On my own?
	GARY	Yes.
115	**HELEN**	What about you?
	GARY	I'll see you there later.
	HELEN	You won't find anything down here, Gary.
	GARY	Yes, I will. See you.

120 *Gary turns and walks off. Helen watches as he recedes into the darkness of the street. She looks at the money in her hand, turns, and walks back up the alley towards the main thoroughfare. We hear the Storyteller's voice.*

STORYTELLER Bright lights, loud music, a sweet smell in the air – the smell of death.

125 *Attention switches to Gary, in the side street. He stands before a lit doorway above which there hangs a sign, 'The Gingerbread Club'. He reads the name aloud.*

GARY 'The Gingerbread Club'.

A voice whispers suddenly nearby.

130 **NICK** Hey!

Gary turns. Nick emerges from a shadow by the side of the doorway. He smiles broadly.

Want to go in?

He holds out his hand.

135 My name's Nick.

Gary stares at Nick.

Be friendly.

Gary shakes Nick's hand. Nick does not let go.

You want to go in there?

140 **GARY** What is it?

NICK You can read, can't you?

GARY 'The Gingerbread Club'. But what is it?

NICK The place your dreams come true.

Gary pulls his hand away from Nick's grasp.

145 **GARY** You're having me on –

He turns away. Nick moves in front of him, still smiling.

NICK I can promise you a good time. Really good, I mean. That's what you're after, isn't it? Something … special. It's special in there, all right.

150 **GARY** What's so special about it?

NICK Go in and find out.

Gary is still hesitant.

7 What do these stage directions suggest about the way the characters are feeling?

8 What body movements could Helen use to show her feelings?

How about a taste?

155 *Nick goes up to the door, opens it. We hear music playing from inside, glimpse a flash of bright, coloured lights. The sight and sound seem to entrance Gary.*

A place of enchantment and delight. Everything you could wish for. And when I say everything … You know what I mean?

Gary is still staring at the lights.

160 Still if you're not interested. *(Nick closes the door.)*

GARY No – I didn't say that – but … how much does it cost?

NICK How much?

GARY To get in.

NICK How much have you got?

165 **GARY** Twenty pounds.

NICK Twenty pounds? Oh, that'll do. That'll do very nicely. More than enough, both for the entrance and the extras.

GARY What extras?

NICK A little bit of spice to make it all nice. *(Nick holds out some pills in*
170 *his hand.)* It's the extras that make it special.

GARY What are they?

NICK They're so new they haven't got a name yet. Call them what you like. Sweeties. Dream-drops. Try one. On the house.

GARY I don't know …

175 *Nick speaks, still smiling, but with more force.*

NICK Try one!

Our attention switches to Storyteller.

STORYTELLER So there he stands at hell's mouth, teetering on the edge, ready to fall in. And no one to help him. No one to take him by the
180 hand, turn him round, guide him back. *(He turns and speaks to Helen, who is standing near him.)*
Is there?

9 What do you think Nick is trying to persuade Gary to try? What is significant about the names he gives to the pills?

	HELEN	What?
	STORYTELLER	Where's your brother?
185	HELEN	My brother? How did you know –?
	STORYTELLER	You look alike. Lost him, have you?
	HELEN	No –
	STORYTELLER	Yes, you have. Or you will do if you don't hurry. Lose him for good.
	HELEN	What do you mean?
190	STORYTELLER	You might be in time, if you hurry.
	HELEN	Go after him. Back … down there …?
	STORYTELLER	Isn't he worth it? Your own brother? Isn't he worth the risk and the danger?
	HELEN	Yes …
195	STORYTELLER	Go on, then. Go on!

Helen turns. Storyteller sniffs.

I can smell something cooking – and it's not the Chinese restaurant.

Attention switches to Gary and Nick outside the club. Gary has taken one of the pills. He is losing control of himself.

200	NICK	Well?
	GARY	Wow!
	NICK	All right?
	GARY	Yeah!
	NICK	Was I right?
205	GARY	Yeah! Right!
	NICK	Takes you up, eh?
	GARY	Way up!
	NICK	Higher and higher!
	GARY	Yeah! Yeah!

10 Stop reading at line 197. Predict what will happen next and how the play will end. Give three reasons, linked to your reading of the play so far and your knowledge of similar stories, for your prediction.

210	**NICK**	Feel that tingling in your fingers, eh? Feel that heat in your bones. And that's only a taste. Only a little taste. In there, it gets hotter. In there, it'll burn you right up!
	GARY	Let's go!
	NICK	You ready?
215	**GARY**	I'm ready. Yeah!
	NICK	Be my guest.
		Nick opens the door. Music and lights again. Gary steps up. Nick stops him, holds out his hand.
		Pay up.
220	**GARY**	Oh, yeah.
		He gives Nick all his money. Nick steps aside.
	NICK	After you.
		Gary steps into the doorway.
	GARY	It's great. It's like … like … I don't know …
225	**NICK**	An oven?
	GARY	What?
		Nick laughs.
		Yeah! Like an oven! Yeah!
		He's about to step in when Helen calls.
230	**HELEN**	Gary!
		Gary turns, sees Helen. He's framed in the doorway with light.
		What are you doing? Where are you going?

> **11** How many references can you find to heat in lines 190–208? What is the significance of this?

	GARY	To paradise. *(to Nick)* Right?
	NICK	Right.
235	**HELEN**	Don't, Gary. You don't know what's in there. It can't be good, whatever it is. Not down here.
	GARY	But it is, Helen. It is good!
	HELEN	It's not! Come on, Gary. Let's go. Please. Let's just go home!
240		*Gary seems to hesitate for a second, then he turns, and disappears into the light.*
		No!
		She takes a step forward. Nick closes the door.
	NICK	Sorry. Too late. *(Nick takes a threatening step towards her.)* Get lost, little girl. Push off. If you know what's good for you. You get
245		my meaning? *(He comes closer to her.)* Unless you want to go in after him. But it'll cost you!
	HELEN	No … no …
		She backs off, turns, and runs down the side street into the dark. Nick looks after her, grinning.
250	**NICK**	Never mind. Another time, maybe. *(He turns and walks back into the shadows.)*
	STORYTELLER	So she runs and leaves him to … whatever waits for him in there. Will she ever know? Will she ever see him again? Probably not. He's just another child taken by the big city, swallowed up and lost
255		for ever. Another child who vanished into the dark behind the bright lights. Of course, if this was a fairytale, she'd have gone in there and saved him, and they'd have gone back home, and lived happily ever after. If this was a fairytale. But it isn't.

12 Look back at your prediction and your reasons for it. Did you pick up clues in the play appropriately? Was there anything that misled you?

The narrator

Sometimes playwrights will use a narrator to help present their ideas. A narrator can have a number of functions in a play. The narrator can:

- set the scene
- tell us what is happening
- interpret what is happening
- comment on the action and the characters
- take on different roles within the play.

Activity 9

1 Note down one example to show how the Storyteller in *Bright Lights* fulfils each of these functions. Your example should include a quotation from the play.

2 Using your examples to help you, write a paragraph explaining the functions of the Storyteller in *Bright Lights*. Where possible, use quotations to support the points you make.

You could start with this sentence:

In Bright Lights the Storyteller has a number of different functions …

Sharpen punctuation

Three-dot ellipsis

The three-dot ellipsis is used to show that something has been omitted or is left unsaid. It can be used:

- for emphasis
- to suggest hesitation in speech
- to create dramatic silences.

The reason for the use of the three-dot ellipsis can sometimes be understood from the context in which it is used. For example, in the following line from *Bright Lights* the three-dot ellipsis is used to suggest that Helen is pointing to different things on the menu:

> **HELEN** We could have that … and that … or that … (line 87)

Find the following lines in *Bright Lights* on pages 148–52. In each case, explain what is being suggested by the use of the three-dot ellipsis:

a HELEN I don't like it. It's dark. It doesn't feel … safe … (line 102)

b NICK And when I say everything … You know what I mean? (line 158)

c GARY It's great. It's like … like … I don't know … (line 224)

Feedback

1 When you have written your paragraph, check that you have used all the relevant information from your notes. If you have missed anything out, add it in.

2 Swap your paragraph with a partner. Has your partner included:
- all the functions of a narrator listed above
- quotations from the play
- all the ideas you did?

If not, jot down the things they didn't include at the end of their work.

3 When your work is returned to you, read the comments your partner has made. Decide if you need to add any details to your paragraph and where they should go.

The playwright's ideas

Here is an outline of the old folk-tale *Hansel and Gretel*, first published by the Brothers Grimm in the early nineteenth century:

> A brother and sister, Hansel and Gretel, are abandoned in the forest by their parents, who are too poor to feed them. Near to starvation, they find a cottage made of bread, cakes and sugar. They are busily eating when an old woman comes out and invites them in. Although they are frightened and have doubts
> 5 about the old woman, they accept her invitation. She turns out to be a witch who imprisons Hansel – with the intention of fattening him up and eating him – and forces Gretel to work for her. When the time comes to bake Hansel in the oven, Gretel tricks the witch into looking in the oven and pushes her inside. The two take the witch's jewels and return home.

 Activity 10

1 Talk about the parallels between *Hansel and Gretel* and *Bright Lights*. Copy the table below and list the ways in which they are similar and different.

Ways in which they are similar	Ways in which they are different
Both stories have two children: a brother and sister.	The children are called Hansel and Gretel in one story and Gary and Helen in the other.

2 When the audience first see Nick he 'emerges from a shadow by the side of the doorway'. Explain how the playwright continues to build a picture of an evil character through:
- the things Nick does
- the things Nick says and the way he says them.

3 When reading *Bright Lights*, you identified several references to heat, for example:

> Feel that heat in your bones. And that's only a taste. Only a little taste. In there, it gets hotter. In there, it'll burn you right up! (lines 210–12)

What other place is suggested by these frequent references to heat?

4 *Bright Lights* ends with the Storyteller saying:

> Of course, if this was a fairytale, she'd have gone in there and saved him, and they'd have gone back home, and lived happily ever after. If this was a fairytale. But it isn't. (lines 256–8)

What message(s) do you think the playwright is trying to get across here? Look back at the table you completed above.

Sharpen spelling

Homophones

Homophones are words which have the same sound but different meanings or different spellings, *wright*, *write*, or *right*, for example. Here are some more examples. Check you know what each word in the pair means.

reed	read	bear	bare	pear	pair
might	mite	bean	been	made	maid

1 With a partner, make a list of as many homophones as you can think of.
2 Compare your list with another pair of students, and add any words they have included which are not on your list.
3 Choose four pairs of homophones. For each pair, write a sentence using both words correctly. You could even join pairs together to make some funny sentences!

Progress check

A script is a particular form of writing. Look back at the range of scripts you have considered in this unit and the work you have done on them.

1 Write an advice sheet for Year 7 students called 'Writing a script'. Use the following sub-headings:
   • When and why you write a script
   • How you can capture characters through the way they speak
   • How you set a script out on the page
   • When and why you use stage directions.

2 Compare your advice with a partner's. Have you missed out anything essential? If your partner offers advice which you don't, add it to your draft.

3 When you have finished your advice sheet, write one of the following sentences at the bottom to show your understanding of how to write a script.

> I'm not sure about more than two of the rules and would like some extra help when I write my own script.
> I'm fairly sure how to do this but may need to look back and check a few things.
> I know how to do this and I'm ready to write my own.

You will soon be writing a short script of your own so it is important you are clear about how to do it.

Assessment task

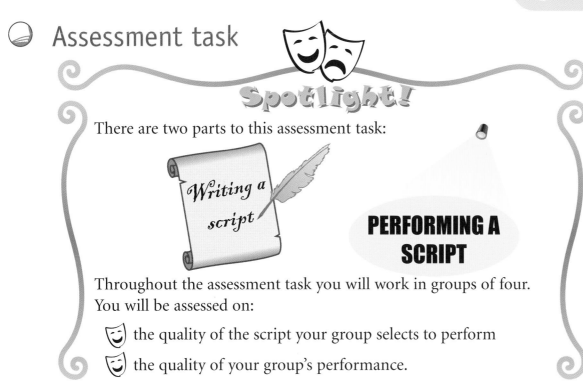

There are two parts to this assessment task:

Writing a script

PERFORMING A SCRIPT

Throughout the assessment task you will work in groups of four. You will be assessed on:

☺ the quality of the script your group selects to perform

☺ the quality of your group's performance.

Writing a script

1 Read the fairy tale, *The Three Wishes* on page 158.

2 Talk about ways in which the fairy tale could be adapted to suit modern times. You need to think about the setting, the characters and the storyline. (Remember you will be performing your script!) Note down as many different ideas as you can.

3 Working in pairs within your group, use your notes to:
- work out a storyline for a script. List the main things that happen in the order in which they happen.
- sketch, or briefly describe, what the three main characters (the elf, the husband, the wife) will be like.
- sketch, or briefly describe, the different settings you would have.
- decide if you want to give your script a particular message, as in *Bright Lights*. If you do, decide how you would make this message clear.

4 Re-read the advice sheet you wrote for Year 7 students about writing a script in the progress check on page 156.

5 Still working in pairs, write the opening 30–60 lines of your playscript.

The Three Wishes

Once upon a time a woodcutter lived happily with his wife in a pretty little log cabin in the middle of a thick forest. One day he came upon a big fir tree with strange holes on the trunk. He was just about to cut it down when the alarmed face of an elf popped out of a hole.

5 'What's all this banging?' asked the elf. 'You're not thinking of cutting down this tree, are you? It's my home.'

The woodcutter dropped his axe in astonishment, but it was not until the elf offered to grant him three wishes that he agreed not to cut the tree down.

When his wife heard of the three wishes she was delighted. 'Hooray! Hooray!
10 Our luck is in,' she shouted and began to picture the wonderful things the elf's wishes might bring them.

Later that evening, they celebrated with a glass of fine wine.

As the woodcutter's wife took a sip she smacked her lips. 'Nice,' she said, ' I wish I had a string of sausages to go with it, though . . .'

15 Instantly she bit her tongue, but it was too late. Out of the air appeared a string of sausages. The woodcutter stuttered with rage.

'What have you done! Sausages. What a foolish waste of a wish! You foolish woman. I wish they would stick to the end of your nose!'

No sooner said than done. The sausages leapt up and stuck fast to the end
20 of the woman's nose. This time the woodcutter's wife flew into a rage.

'You idiot! With all the things we could have wished for!'

At first the woodcutter was mortified but, as his wife continued to shout at him, he burst out laughing.

'If only you knew how funny you look with those sausages on the end of
25 your nose.'

Now that really upset the woodcutter's wife. She hadn't thought about how she might look. Terrified, she exclaimed, 'What shall I do? They'll be there for the rest of my life!'

The woodcutter felt sorry for his wife. Together
30 they tried to pull the sausages from her nose but it was no use. The pair sat on the floor, gazing sadly at each other.

'I'm afraid there's only one thing we can do …' said the
35 woodcutter. 'I wish the sausages would leave my wife's nose.'

And they did. Instantly. Husband and wife
40 hugged each other tearfully, saying 'Maybe we'll be poor, but we'll be happy again!'

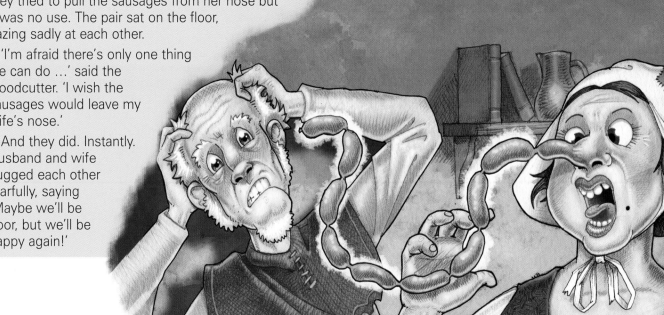

Performing a script

6 a Working in your group of four, read and assess each pair's script. Decide which one would be the most interesting to perform and to watch. To help you decide, think about how the writers have:

- captured the characters through the way they speak
- used stage directions to make clear what is happening and how the characters should move and talk
- made their script interesting.

b When you have made your choice, talk about any improvements that could be made to the script to make it as good as possible. Make these improvements.

7 Choose one person to be the director of the performance. This person will give you advice on:

- how you should say the words
- the facial expressions and body movements you should make.

It is very important that the actors listen to, and follow, the advice of the director.

8 Use what you learnt from the progress check on page 144 to help you decide:

- who should play each part and why
- the most important things about this scene and how you will bring them out.

9 Learn your lines as this helps the performance flow more easily.

10 Present your performance to another group of students or the whole class. Remember to:

- stay in role throughout the performance
- say your words clearly, using appropriate tone of voice
- match your facial expressions and body movements to the words.

Heinemann is an imprint of Pearson Education Limited,
a company incorporated in England and Wales, having
its registered office at Edinburgh Gate, Harlow, Essex, CM20 2JE.
Registered company number: 872828

Heinemann is a registered trademark of Pearson Education Limited
© Harcourt Education Limited, 2005

First published 2005

12

10

British Library Cataloguing in Publication Data is available from the British Library on request.

ISBN: 978 0 435227 30 2

Copyright notice

All rights reserved. No part of this publication may be reproduced in any form or by any means (including photocopying or storing it in any medium by electronic means and whether or not transiently or incidentally to some other use of this publication) without the written permission of the copyright owner, except in accordance with the provisions of the Copyright, Designs and Patents Act 1988 or under the terms of a licence issued by the Copyright Licensing Agency, 90 Tottenham Court Road, London W1T 4LP. Applications for the copyright owner's written permission should be addressed to the publisher.

Cover design by Wooden Ark Studio   Designed by Wooden Ark Studio   Printed and bound in China (CTPS/10)
Cover photo: © Getty   Produced by Kamae Design

Original illustrations © Harcourt Education Limited 2005

Illustrated by **Johanna Boccardo:** pp16–17, 30, 40–41, 42, 58b, 139; **Chris Brown:** pp33, 121, 122; **Andy Elkerton:** pp8, 44, 48–49, 158; **Alice Englander:** pp105, 136; **Phil Healey:** pp7 (Fig 5), 14, 21, 43, 58; **Andrew Morris:** pp9, 103, 123, 124; **John Storey:** pp 6, 7

Photos: pp11, 29, 36, 52, 59, 61**L**, 75, 78, 109, 112, 115, 116, 118, 131, 132, 134**T3**, 134**M2**, 134**M3**, 134**B**, 140, 143**L**, 152, 153 Corbis; pp13**L**, 55 Cumulus; p13**M**, 134**M1**, 143**R** Getty Images/Photodisc; pp13**R**, 83**B**, 86 NHPA; p18 BBC Photo Archive; p19 Getty Images; pp22, 61**R**, 81, 142, 146–151 Rex; p38 Harcourt Education Ltd/Tudor Photography; p61**M** BBC Picture Library; pp68, 90 Ronald Grant; p69**R** Walt Disney Pictures/The Kobal Collection; p83**T** Topham Picturepoint; p110 Moviestore; p123 Fortean Picture Library; p125 Rexfeatures; pp126, 134**T2** Copyright © BBC; p134**T1** Peter Evans/Cumulus.

Acknowledgements

Every effort has been made to contact copyright holders of material reproduced in this book. Any omissions will be rectified in subsequent printings if notice is given to the publishers.

Extract from 'An eight-foot howling yeti' by Ian Valentine, Country Life January 24th 2003. Copyright © Ian Valentine/Country Life/IPC Syndication. Reprinted with permission of IPC Syndication; 'Checking Out Me History' by John Agard, from *Life Doesn't Frighten Me At All: Poems* published by Henry Holt 1989. Copyright © 1996 by John Agard. Reproduced by kind permission of John Agard c/o Caroline Sheldon Literary Agency Ltd; extracts from ICI paint chart: English Forest, Paradise Blue, Roasted Red, Happy Violet and Babe are trademarks of Imperial Chemical Industries PLC in the United Kingdom and used with their kind permission; extract from *A Kestrel for a Knave* by Barry Hines, Penguin 1969. Copyright © Barry Hines 1969. Reprinted with permission of Penguin Books Ltd; extract from 'Search for survivors after factory blast' by Gerard Seenan and Kirsty Scott, *The Guardian*, 12th May 2004. Copyright © Guardian Newspapers Ltd 2004. Used with permission; extract from *The Rough Guide to Canada*. Reprinted with permission of Rough Guides Ltd; extract from 'Service with a snarl' by Jeanette Hyde, *The Observer*, 27th May 2001. Copyright © Guardian Newspapers Ltd 2001. Used with permission; extracts from 'Into the Heart of Borneo' by Redmond O'Hanlon, published by Random House, Inc. Copyright © by Francis Russell. Reprinted by permission of Sll/Sterling Lord Literistic, Inc; *The Gift* by Ray Bradbury. Copyright © 1952 by Esquire, Inc., renewed 1980 by Ray Bradbury. Reprinted by permission of Don Congdon Associates Inc.; 'Stars and Planets' by Norman MacCaig. Reproduced by permission of Polygon, an imprint of Birlinn Ltd; extract from *The Crocodile Hunter* by Steve and Terri Irwin. Copyright © by Steve Irwin and Terri Irwin 2001. Reprinted by permission of The Orion Publishing Group Ltd, Penguin Group Australia, and Dutton, a division of Penguin Putnam Group (USA) Inc.; posters 'pack of lies' and 'hairy tongue' Copyright © GASP. Reprinted with permission; Warwick Castle Ghosts Alive poster. Reprinted with the kind permission of Warwick Castle; review of Philip Pullman's *His Dark Materials* by Guy Macdonald. Copyright © Guy Macdonald. Reprinted with the kind permission of the author; review of the film *Peter Pan* taken from *DVD Review*, Issue 64. Reprinted with the kind permission of Paragon; front cover of PC game *Football Manager 2005* used with the kind permission of SEGA Europe; Wag & Bone Show article, *Dogs Today*, July 2004. Reprinted with permission; 'Become an Organ Donor' speech by David Slack of speeches.com. Copyright © Instant Speeches Ltd. Reprinted with the kind permission of the author; extract from 'A Large order of fries and 500 gallons of water - To Go' reprinted with permission from *Windows on the Wild – A Biodiversity Primer*. Copyright © 2002. A publication of World Wildlife Fund's 'Window on the Wild' biodiversity education program. For more information please visit www.worldwildlife.org/windows; article 'Fox attacks girl in her bedroom 'by Geoff Maynard, *The Daily Express*, 5th September 2003. Copyright © Express Newspapers. Reprinted with permission; article 'Disaster film reigns at flicks this week', *Stockport Times East*, Thursday 27th May 2004. Reprinted with permission; extract from Castleton leaflet. Reproduced by the kind permission of the Castleton Chamber of Trade; extract from *Success! ICT at KS3* by Gareth Williams, Pearson 2002. Copyright © Pearson Publishing 2002; extract from *Living Through History Book 1: The Roman Empire* by Nigel Kelly, Rosemary Rees and Jane Shuter. Published by Heinemann Educational 1997; extract from *Eureka! 3R* by Carol Chapman, Rob Musker, Daniel Nicholson and Moira Sheehan. Published by Heinemann Educational 2001; extracts of text (adapted) and illustrations from *Horrible Science: Disgusting Digestion* by Nick Arnold, illustrated by Tony de Saulles, published by Scholastic in 1998. Text copyright © Nick Arnold 1998. Illustrations copyright © Tony de Saulles 1998; extract from the *Illustrated Family Encyclopedia*. Copyright © 1975–1987 Marshall Cavendish Ltd. Reprinted with their kind permission; extract from 'The Battle of Hastings', found at www.britainexpress.com. Reprinted with permission; extracts from *The Whale Rider* by Witi Ihimaera. Published by Reed Books, a division of Reed Publishing (NZ) Ltd. Copyright © Witi Ihimaera 1987. Reprinted with the kind permission of Reed Publishing (NZ) Ltd; 'Killing a Whale' by David Gill, *Axed Between the Ears* published by Heinemann Educational 1987; extract from *Whale Nation* by Heathcote Williams, published by Jonathan Cape. Used by permission of The Random House Group Ltd; Loch Ness Monster extracts from www.sansilke.freeserve.co.uk and www.myspace.co.uk; 'The Loch Ness Monster's Song' by Edwin Morgan from *Collected Poems* published by Carcanet Press. Reprinted by permission of Carcanet Press Ltd; 'New Nessie pictures spark debate' by Stephen Fraser, *The Scotsman* 22nd September 2004. Reprinted with permission of The Scotsman Publications Ltd; 'BBC "Proves" Nessie does not exist'. Taken from http://news.bbc.co.uk/2/hi/science/nature/3096839.stm. Copyright © BBC. Reprinted by permission of the BBC; extract about oil pollution from www.yptenc.org.uk. Reprinted with permission; extracts from www.oceana.org. Reprinted with permission; 'New Zealanders save some whales in mass standing' by Ray Lilley, Associated Press, 8th January 2003. Reprinted with permission; 'North Sea Cod at crisis point' by Alex Kirby, Sunday 15th June 2004. Taken from http://news.bbc.co.uk/1/hi/sci/tech/2987682.stm. Copyright © BBC. Reprinted with permission of the BBC; extract from www.mcsuk.org about Volunteer Projects with MCS. Reprinted with permission; extracts from *Scripts and Sketches*, edited by John O'Connor. Published by Heinemann Educational Publishers 2001: 'The Bully' by Gene Kemp, 'The Mobile' by Mark Morris. Copyright © Mark Morris 2001. Reprinted with the kind permission of the author, 'Joyride' by Steve Barlow and Steve Skidmore, 'The Off-side trap' by Mary Colson. Copyright © Mary Colson 2001. Reprinted with the kind permission of the author; 'Bright Lights' by David Calcutt. Copyright © David Calcutt 2001. Reprinted with the kind permission of the author; activities for 'Bright Lights' by David Calcutt. Activities by and copyright © to John O'Connor 2001. Reprinted by permission of the author.